FOR THE TURNED ON, TUNED IN
AND DROPPED OUT

LOVE

The Beatles, 1967

FREAK OUT HEAVY MIND
BLAST DUDE EASY
CRUISING BREWSKI
FINK WHAT'S YOUR BAG?
WICKED GNARLY TRIPPY
HANG OUT RIGHT ON
CHOICE HEP CHICK
CHERRY OUTTA'

BENDING BUMMER BAD
WIPE OUT LOADED
HANG LOOSE PRIMO
FUNKY GROOVY HANGIN'
FAR OUT FLAKE BADASS
COOL FAB BLITZED
MAKING THE SCENE
SIGHT RIGHTEOUS

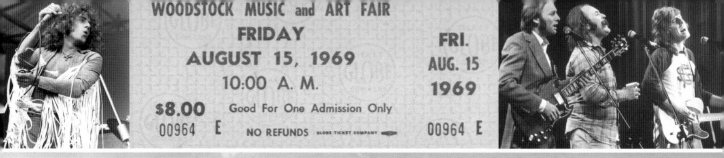

WOODSTOCK MUSIC and ART FAIR
FRIDAY
AUGUST 15, 1969
10:00 A. M.

FRI.
AUG. 15
1969

$8.00   Good For One Admission Only
00964 E   NO REFUNDS   GLOBE TICKET COMPANY

00964 E

"Good morning! What we have in mind is breakfast in bed

for 400,000. "

Wavy Gravy, Woodstock

GENTLE PATH

GROOVY WAY →

← HIGH WAY

WOODSTOCK
MUSIC & ART FAIR
presents
AN
AQUARIAN
EXPOSITION
in
WHITE LAKE, N.Y.

WITH
FRI., AUG. 15
Joan Baez
Arlo Guthrie
Tim Hardin
Richie Havens
Incredible String Band
Ravi Shankar
Sly And The Family Stone
Bert Sommer
Sweetwater

SAT., AUG. 16
Canned Heat
Creedence Clearwater
Grateful Dead
Keef Hartley
Janis Joplin
Jefferson Airplane
Mountain
Quill
Santana
The Who

SUN., AUG. 17
The Band
Jeff Beck Group
Blood, Sweat and Tears
Joe Cocker
Crosby, Stills and Nash
Paul Hendis
Iron Butterfly
Ten Years After
Johnny Winter

ART SHOW

CRAFTS BAZAAR

FOOD

HUNDREDS OF ACRES
TO ROAM ON

MUSIC STARTS AT 4:00 P.M. ON
FRIDAY AND AT 1:00 P.M. ON
SATURDAY AND SUNDAY.

**AUGUST
15, 16, 17**

3 DAYS
of PEACE
& MUSIC

*WHITE LAKE, TOWN OF BETHEL, SULLIVAN COUNTY, N.Y.

STEVE McQUEEN

The MIRISCH COMPANY Presents

Steve McQUEEN · James GARNER · Richard ATTENBOROUGH

A GLORIOUS SAGA OF THE R.A.F

JOHN STURGES'

COLOUR BY DE LUXE
PANAVISION®

THE GREAT ESCAPE

JAMES **DONALD** · CHARLES **BRONSON** · DONALD **PLEASENCE** · JAMES **COBURN** · JOHN **LEYTON** · Produced & Directed by JOHN **STURGES** · Screenplay by JAMES **CLAVELL** & W.R. **BURNETT** · Based upon the book by PAUL **BRICKHILL**

Music by ELMER BERNSTEIN · A MIRISCH-ALPHA PICTURE · UNITED ARTISTS

The Magnificent Seven	1960	Baby, the Rain Must Fall	1965
The Honeymoon Machine	1961	The Cincinnati Kid	1965
Hell is for Heroes	1962	The Sand Pebbles	1966
The War Lovers	1962	Nevada Smith	1966
The Great Escape	1963	The Thomas Crown Affair	1968
Soldier in the Rain	1963	Bullitt	1968
Love with the Proper Stranger	1963	The Reivers	1969

"When a horse learns to buy martinis, I'll learn to like horses."

STEVE McQUEEN

the KING of COOL

"Come on everybody clap your hands
Now you're looking good
I'm gonna sing my song and you won't take long
We gotta do the twist and it goes like this

THE TWIST

Come on let's twist again like we did last summer
Yea, let's twist again like we did last year
Do you remember when things were really hummin'
Yea, let's twist again, twistin' time is here."

THREE STEPS

AD LIB

1
STANCE: Prizefighter position, one leg extended forward and arms extended forward from the elbow.

2
MOVEMENT: Hips swivel from side to side as if rubbing oneself with a towel. Knees are bent slightly. As hips move left, arms move to the right, and vice versa.

3
FOOT MOVEMENT: Twist fast as if putting out a cigarette. Entire body moves forward and back and from side to side.

4
DEEP BEND STEP: Bend knees as far as possible, then rise. Repeat motion.

5
LASSO STEP: Extend one arm over the head and twirl as if throwing a lasso.

6
FORWARD STEP: While twisting, lift one foot off the ground and return to place. Repeat motion.

...like this... ...goes it and... we're gonna' do the TWIST

PSYCHE

With the influence of LSD, psychedelia gave birth to an explosion of colorful and mind-blowing artwork,

Throughout the 1960s, five artists dominated the psychedelic rock poster art scene and were known as the "Big Five": Wes Wilson, Stanley Mouse, Alton Kelley, Rick Griffin (originally a surf artist and creator of "Murph the Surf," Rick's most famous poster is The Grateful Dead's Aoxomoxoa) and Victor Moscoso.

Wilson

Mouse

Griffin

Moscoso

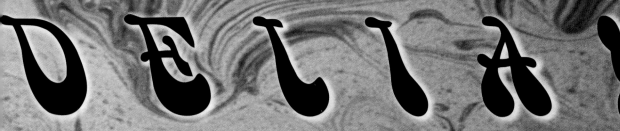

DELIA!

Max

One of the most influential psychedelic artists of the 1960s, Peter Max's famous "Cosmic '60s" – with its distinctive line work, bold color combinations and transcendental imagery – captured the imagination of the hippie generation.

particularly on posters and handbills that were created to promote dances and concerts.

Spiegelman

Underground Comics

Underground comics were self-published or small press comic books that sprang up in the 1960s, originating in San Francisco. Prominent artists associated with underground comics included Robert Crumb, Robert Williams, S. Clay Wilson, Rick Griffin, Gilbert Shelton, Art Spiegelman and Kim Deitch.

Titles included: The Fabulous Furry Freak Brothers, Air Pirates Funnies, Arcade, Bijou Funnies, Binky Brown Meets the Holy Virgin Mary, Bogeyman, Coochie Cootie's Men's Comics, Corn Fed, Hytone, Despair, Big Ass, XYZ, It Ain't Me Babe, Tales from the Tube, Wimmen's Comix and Zap.

"I'm so mean I make medicine sick."

The Greatest.

"If you even dream of beating me you'd better wake up and apologize."

"Float like a butterfly, sting like a bee
His hands can't hit what his eyes can't see."

"I done wrassled with an alligator ‧
I done tussled with a whale
Only last week I murdered a rock
Injured a stone, hospitalized a brick
I'm so mean I make medicine sick."

Cassius Marcellus Clay
aka Muhammad Ali

1960
Sep. 5 Won the gold medal in the Light Heavyweight division against Zbigniew Pietrzykowski at the Rome Olympics
Oct. 29 Tunney Hunsaker, Louisville, Kentucky, W6 (first professional fight)
Dec. 27 Herb Siler, Miami Beach, Florida, KO4

1961
Jan. 17 Anthony Sperti, Miami Beach, Florida, KO3
Feb. 7 Jim Robinson, Miami Beach, Florida, KO1
Feb. 21 Donnie Fleeman, Miami Beach, Florida, KO7
Apr. 19 Lamar Clark, Louisville, Kentucky, KO2
Jun. 26 Duke Sabedong, Las Vegas, Nevada, W10
Jul. 22 Alonzo Johnson, Louisville, Kentucky, W10
Oct. 7 Alex Miteff, Louisville, Kentucky, KO6
Nov. 29 Willie Besmanoff, Louisville, Kentucky, KO7

1962
Feb. 10 Sonny Banks, New York, New York, KO4
Feb. 28 Don Warner, Miami Beach, Florida, KO4
Apr. 23 George Logan, Los Angeles, California, KO6
May 19 Billy Daniels, New York, New York, KO7
Jul. 20 Alejandro Lavorante, Los Angeles, California, KO5
Nov. 15 Archie Moore, Los Angeles, California, KO4

1963
Jan. 24 Charlie Powell, Pittsburgh, Pennsylvania, KO3
Mar. 13 Doug Jones, New York, New York, W10
Jun. 18 Henry Cooper, London, England, KO5

1964
Feb. 25 Sonny Liston, Miami Beach, Florida, TKO7 (World Heavyweight Champion)
Feb. 26 Announces his conversion to Islam and is given the name **"Muhammad Ali"**

1965
May 25 Sonny Liston, Lewiston, Maine, KO1 (retains World Heavyweight Champion title)
Nov. 22 Floyd Patterson, Las Vegas, Nevada, KO12 (retains World Heavyweight Champion title)

1966
Mar. 29 George Chuvalo, Toronto, Canada, W15 (retains World Heavyweight Champion title)
May 21 Henry Cooper, London, England, KO6 (retains World Heavyweight Champion title)
Aug. 6 Brian London, London, England, KO3 (retains World Heavyweight Champion title)
Sep. 10 Karl Mildenberger, Frankfurt, Germany, KO12 (retains World Heavyweight Champion title)
Nov. 14 Cleveland Williams, Houston, Texas, KO3 (retains World Heavyweight Champion title)

1967
Feb. 6 Ernie Terrell, Houston, Texas, W15 (retains World Heavyweight Champion title)
Mar. 22 Zora Folley, New York, New York, KO7 (retains World Heavyweight Champion title)

"The People's Car"

Is Volkswagen contemplating a change?

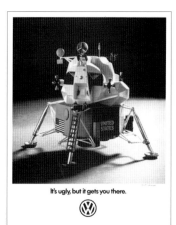

It's ugly, but it gets you there.

Think small.

In 5 minutes it had better turn into a station wagon.

John Fitzgerald Kennedy

1917 – 1963

"I look forward
to an America
which will not be
afraid of grace
and beauty."

"And so, my fellow
Americans: ask not
what your country
can do for you –
ask what you can
do for your country.
My fellow citizens
of the world: ask
not what America
will do for you,
but what together
we can do for the
freedom of man."

Inaugural address, January 20, 1961

35th President of the United States of America

John Fitzgerald Kennedy and Jacqueline Lee Bouvier were married on September 12, 1953. In 1957, Caroline Bouvier Kennedy was born and John Fitzgerald Kennedy Jr. (known as John-John) followed in 1960.

On November 22, 1963, hardly past his first thousand days in office, John Fitzgerald Kennedy was killed by an assassin's bullets as his motorcade rode through Dallas, Texas.

"From Dallas, Texas, a flash, apparently official. President Kennedy died at 1PM, central standard time, two o'clock eastern standard time, some thirty-eight minutes ago."

CBS' Walter Kronkite, visibly emotional, announces the news

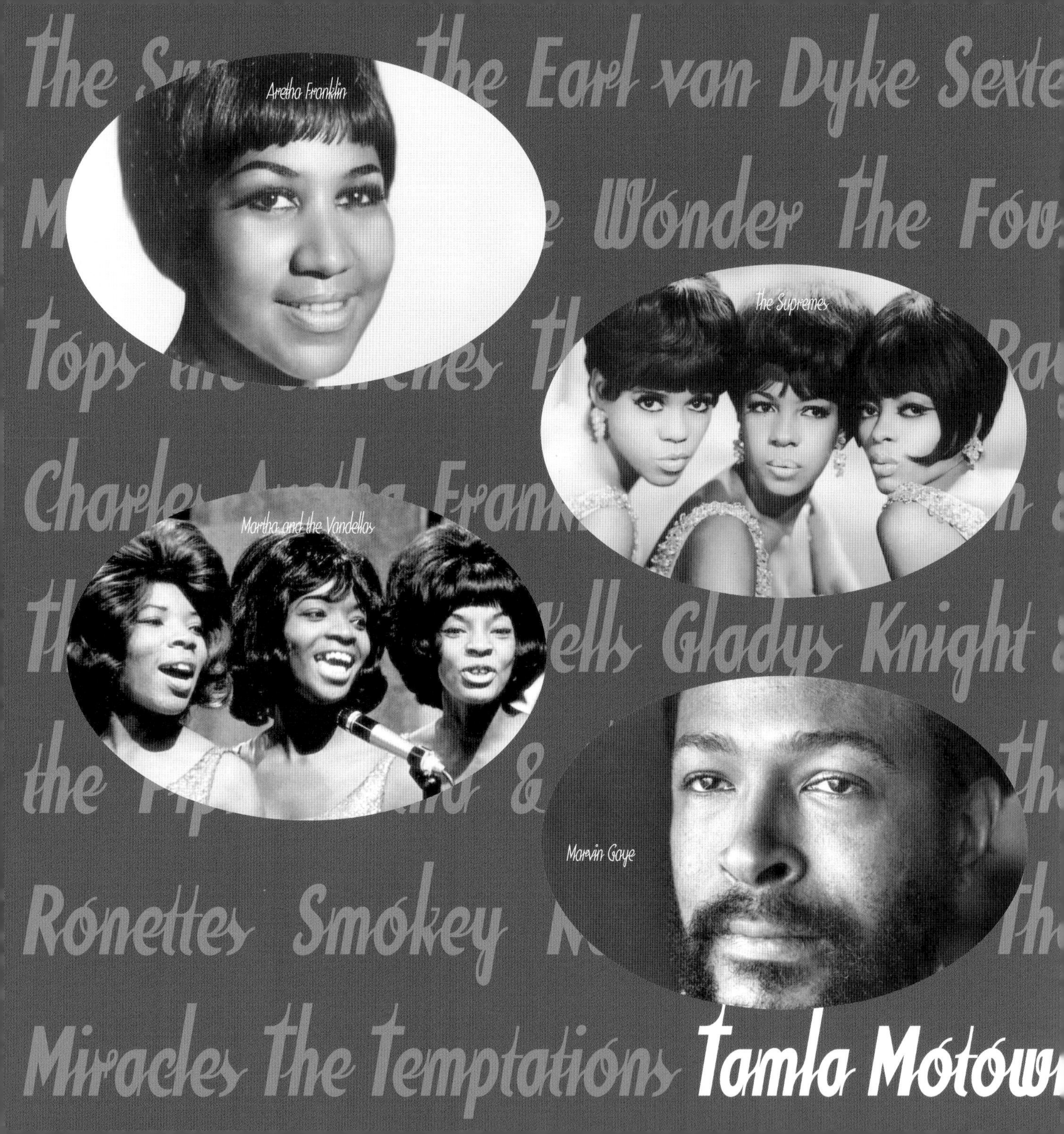

Aretha Franklin
The Supremes
Martha and the Vandellas
Marvin Gaye
the Earl van Dyke
Wonder The
Tops
Gladys Knight
the
Ronettes Smokey
Miracles the Temptations
Tamla

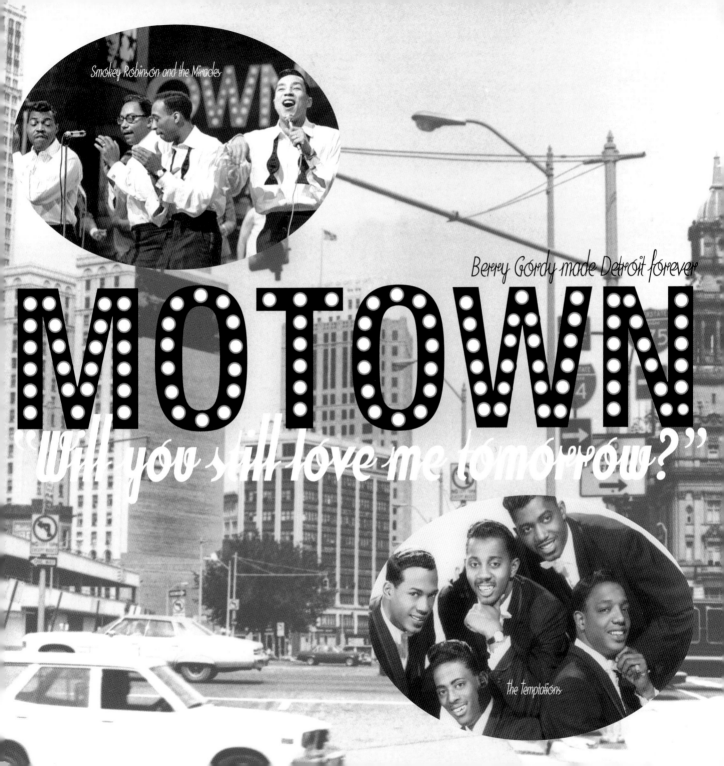

Smokey Robinson and the Miracles

Berry Gordy made Detroit forever

MOTOWN

"Will you still love me tomorrow?"

the Temptations

FREE LOVE

anyone...

1960

DH Lawrence's 1928 novel, *Lady Chatterley's Lover*, is published in the UK in its entirety for the first time.

1960

The contraceptive pill is approved by the FDA.

1962

The first James Bond film, *Dr. No*, is released, introducing the trademark "Bond girls" (Honey Ryder and Sylvia Trench who are followed by Pussy Galore in *Goldfinger* and Kissy Suzuki in *You Only Live Twice*).

anywhere...

anytime!

1963

John Cleland's 1750 novel *Fanny Hill* is published by G.B. Putnam under the title *John Cleland's Memoirs of a Woman of Pleasure* and is immediately banned for obscenity. After challenging the ban in court, the publisher wins a landmark decision in 1966 when the United States Supreme Court rules that the novel does not meet the Roth standard for obscenity.

1965

Penthouse magazine is founded.

1966

The Human Sexual Response by Dr. William Masters and Dr. Virginia Johnson is published.

1967

The first "Human Be-In" is held in San Francisco, beginning "The Summer of Love."

1969

The Way to Become The Sensuous Woman by Joan Garrity (identifying herself only as "J") is published and includes things such as exercises for improving the dexterity of the tongue.

1969

Everything You Always Wanted to Know About Sex (But Were Afraid to Ask) by David Reuben, M.D., is published.

1969

Full-frontal nudity appears in *Playboy* magazine for the first time.

It's Ma

Bewitched
September 17, 1964 – August 1, 1972

Cast

Elizabeth Montgomery – **Samantha (& Serena)**

Dick York/Dick Sargent – **Darrin**

Agnes Moorhead – **Endora**

David White – **Larry Tate**

Erin Murphy and Diane Murphy – **Tabitha Stevens** (1966-1972)

gic!

I DREAM OF JEANNIE

September 18, 1965 – September 1, 1970

"Yes master?"

Cast

Barbara Eden – Jeannie

Larry Hagman – Captain (& later, Major) Anthony Nelson

Bill Daily – Captain (& later, Major) Roger Healey

Hayden Rorke – Colonel Alfred E. Bellows M.D.

Jeannie: "But master, I only did it to please you."

Major Nelson and Jeannie marry on December 2, 1969

FLOWER CHILDREN

incense

Bohemian

Love beads

Batik

Love-ins

PEACE

Headbands

LOVE

Kaftans

Sit-ins

Beatnik

Sandals

Tie-Dye

Bell Bottoms

Meditation

GOOD VIBES

The Beatles

"The Ed Sullivan Show," February 9, 1964

When the news was announced that the Beatles were going to appear on "The Ed Sullivan Show," the CBS Television office in New York was overwhelmed by more than 50,000 requests for tickets to a studio that held only 700.

Ringo Starr
(b. Richard Starkey, 1940)

George Harold Harrison
(1943 – 2001)

John Winston Lennon
(1940 – 1980)

James Paul McCartney
(b. 1942)

73 million people tuned in to watch The Beatles and mass hysteria resulted wherever they appeared – "Beatlemania" had arrived.

"It was crazy.
Not within the band.

Their first UK single was Love Me Do/P.S. I Love You, released October 5, 1962, by EMI/Parlophone Records.

Their first USA single was Please Please Me/Ask Me Why, released on February 25, 1963 by Vee Jay Records. It was their fourth single however, I Want To Hold Your Hand/I Saw Her Standing There, released on December 26, 1963, that was The Beatles' first US hit. It went to Number 1 on the Billboard Charts on January 18, 1964, and stayed there for seven weeks.

During their recording career from 1962 to 1970, the Beatles recorded 214 songs and released 22 singles in the UK and 33 in the USA.

Albums

Please, Please Me (UK, 1963)
Introducing The Beatles (USA, 1963)
With The Beatles (1963 – released as Meet the Beatles in the USA)
A Hard Day's Night (1964)
Beatles For Sale (1964 – released as Beatles '65 in the USA)
Rubber Soul (1965)
Revolver (1966)
Sgt. Pepper's Lonely Hearts Club Band (1967)
The White Album (1968)
Yellow Submarine (1969)
Abbey Road (1969)
Let It Be (1970)

Films

A Hard Day's Night (1964)
Help (1965)
Magical Mystery Tour (1967)
Yellow Submarine (USA only, 1968)

In the band we were normal, and the rest of the world was crazy."
George Harrison

Stage Fright

Strangers on a Train

I Confess

Dial M for Murder

Rear Window

To Catch a Thief

Vertigo

North by Northwest

Psycho

The Birds

Marnie

Torn Curtain

Topaz

PSYCHO

"Always make the audience
suffer as much as possible."

Alfred Hitchcock

On his mission in life:
"To simply scare the hell out
of people."

To crew complaints that Tallulah Bankhead's habit of not wearing any underpants was creating camera angle problems in shooting *Lifeboat*: "I don't know if this is a matter for the costume department or the hairdresser."

"Seeing a murder on television can help work off one's antagonisms. And if you haven't any antagonisms, the commericals will give you some."

When an actress asked Hitchcock if her right or left profile was better, he told her, "My dear, you're sitting on your best profile."

"The length of a film should be directly related to the endurance of the human bladder."

Spies

Movies

The Manchurian Candidate
1962

The Spy Who Came In
From The Cold
1965

The Ipcress File
1965

The Man
From U.N.C.L.E.
1964 – 1968

U.N.C.L.E. – United Network
Command for Law Enforcement.
T.H.R.U.S.H. – Technological
Hierarchy for the Removal of
Undesirables and the
Subjugation of Humanity.

Robert Vaughan –
Napoleon Solo

David McCallum –
Illya Kuryakin

Leo G. Carroll –
Alexander Waverly

Barbara Moore –
Lisa Rogers
(1967–1968)

Get Smart
1965 – 1970

"Sorry about that Chief."

Don Adams – **Maxwell Smart, Agent 86**

Barbara Feldon – **Agent 99**

Edward Platt – **The Chief**

William Schallart – **Admiral Harold**
Harmon Hargrade (1967–1968)

Bernie Kopell – **Conrad Siegfried**
(1966–1969)

King Moody – **Starker (1967–1969)**

Joey Forman – **Harry Hoo (1966)**

Victor French – **Agent 44 (1965–1966)**

Richard Gautier – **Hypie the Robot**
(1966–1969)

Robert Karvelas – **Larrabee (1967–1970)**

Stacy Keach Sr. – **Carlson (1966–1967)**

David Ketchum – **Agent 13 (1966–1967)**

Al Molinaro – **Agent 44 (1969–1970)**

The Avengers 1961 – 1969

"Mrs Peel, we're needed."

Patrick Macnee – **John Steed**

Honor Blackman – **Cathy Gale (1962–1964)**

Julie Stevens – **Venus Smith (1962–1963)**

Diana Rigg – **Emma Peel (1965–1967)**

Linda Thorson – **Tara King (1968–1969)**

Rhonda Parker – **Rhonda (1966–1969)**

Patrick Newell – **Mother (1968–1969)**

Mission Impossible 1966 – 1973

"Your mission, Jim, should you decide to accept it...
As usual, should you or any of your I.M. Force be captured or killed,
the Secretary will disavow any knowledge of your existence.
This tape will self-destruct in five seconds. Good luck, Jim."

Peter Graves – **Jim Phelps**
Greg Morris – **Barney Collier**
Peter Lupus – **Willy Armitage**
Barbara Bain – **Cinnamon Carter (1966–1969)**
Martin Landau – **Rollin Hand (1966–1969)**
Leonard Nimoy – **Paris (1969–1971)**
Steven Hill – **Daniel Briggs (1966–1967)**

I Spy 1965 – 1968

Robert Culp – **Kelly Robinson**
Bill Cosby – **Alexander Scott**
Antoinette Bower – **Shelby Clavell**
Sheldon Leonard – **Sorgi**
France Nuyen – **Sam-than McLean**
Alan Oppenheimer – **Colonel Benkovsky**
Harold Stone – **Zarkas**
Kenneth Tobey – **Russ Conway**

MARTIN LUTHER

"I have a dream

that my four children will one day live in a nation where they will not be judged by the color of their skin, but by the content of their character..."

1963 *Time Magazine* "Man of the Year"
1964 Nobel Peace Price

KING, JR. 1929-1968

"We've got some difficult days ahead. But it doesn't really matter with me now, because I've been to the mountaintop and I don't mind... I just want to do God's will, and he's allowed me to go up to the mountain... I've looked over and I've seen **the promised land.**"

Sermon, April 3, 1968

"I have bad news for you; for all of our fellow citizens; and that is that Martin Luther King was shot and killed tonight."

Robert F. Kennedy speaking to a crowd in Indiana, April 4, 1968

SINCE 1896 S&H GREEN STAMPS

Remember Green Stamps?

Sperry & Hutchinson, distributor of S&H Green Stamps, started offering stamps to retailers in 1896. The retail organizations bought the stamps from S&H and gave them away with every purchase based on the amount you spent. The more you spent, the more stamps you received. When you'd saved up enough stamps you could trade them in for merchandise at a local redemption center or order via a catalog.

S&H ran the most successful program and in the mid-60s were the largest purchaser of consumer products in the world, printing three times as many stamps as the US Postal Service, and their catalog was possibly the largest single publication in the country.

You could get anything from toasters to life insurance policies, and a lot of fundraising relied on stamps – a school in Erie, Pennsylvania, even saved up 5.4 million Green Stamps to buy a pair of gorillas for the local zoo!

"*I'm dollars ahead—thanks to S&H Green Stamps*" *says* **MRS. DONALD R. MAYNE,** *La Jolla housewife*

Different colored stamps were available from different stamp companies – ORANGE, YELLOW, K&S RED, PINKY, BLUE CHIP and PLAID; TOP VALUE, MOR-VALU, SHUR-VALU, BIG BONUS and DOUBLE THRIFT; BUCKEYE, BUCCANEER, TWO GUYS, KING CORN and EAGLE; and REGAL.

CLEOPATRA

"SURELY THE MOST BIZARRE PIECE OF ENTERTAINMENT TO BE PERPETUATED."
ELIZABETH TAYLOR

"The long-awaited 20th Century Fox production of *Cleopatra* will go down in film history as the most opulent, pictorially magnificent and eye-filling screen spectacle ever made…

Probably no other present-day actress could equal the regal beauty and fiery dramatic talents of Elizabeth Taylor, who portrays Cleopatra…"

Review, June 17, 1963

Elizabeth Taylor met Richard Burton during the filming of *Cleopatra*. Elizabeth divorced fourth husband, Eddie Fisher, on March 6, 1964, and married Richard Burton on March 15, 1964. The Vatican denounced their behavior during the filming of *Cleopatra* as "erotic vagrancy."

THE UNTOUCHABLES 1959 - 1963

ABEL FERNANDEZ - AGENT WILLIAM YOUNGFELLOW

NICHOLAS GEORGIADE - AGENT ENRICO ROSSI

BRUCE GORDON - FRANK NITTI

STEVE LONDON - AGENT JACK ROSSMAN

JERRY PARIS - AGENT MARTIN FLAHERTY (1959-1960)

ROBERT STACK - ELIOT NESS

FRANK WILCOX - DISTRICT ATTORNEY BEECHER ASBURY

WALTER WINCHELL - NARRATOR

THE MOD SQUAD 1964 - 1973

PEGGY LIPTON - JULIE BARNES

CLARENCE WILLIAMS III - LINCOLN "LINC" HAYES

MICHAEL COLE - PETE COCHRAN

TIGE ANDREWS - CAPTAIN ADAM GREER

THE FUGITIVE 1963 - 1967

DAVID JANSSEN - DR. RICHARD KIMBLE

BARRY MORSE - LT. PHILIP GERARD

BILL RAISCH - FRED JOHNSON (THE ONE-ARMED MAN)

DIANE BREWSTER (FLASHBACKS) - HELEN KIMBLE

J.D. CANNON - LLOYD CHANDLER

WILLIAM CONRAD - NARRATOR (VOICE)

HANK SIMMS - INTRODUCTORY NARRATOR

IRONSIDE 1967 - 1975

RAYMOND BURR - ROBERT T. IRONSIDE

DON GALLOWAY - DETECTIVE SERGEANT ED BROWN

DON MITCHELL - MARK SANGER

BARBARA ANDERSON - EVE WHITFIELD (1967-1971)

GENE LYONS - COMMISSIONER DENNIS RANDALL

JOHNNY SEVEN - LIEUTENANT CAL REESE (1969-1975)

F.B.I. 1965 - 1974

EFREM ZIMBALIST JR. - INSPECTOR LEWIS ERSKINE

PHILIP ABBOTT - ASSISTANT DIRECTOR ARTHUR WARD

STEPHEN BROOKS - SPECIAL AGENT JIM RHODES (1965-1967)

WILLIAM REYNOLDS - SPECIAL AGENT TOM COLBY (1967-1973)

LYNN LORING - BARBARA ERSKINE (1965-1966)

CAR 54, WHERE ARE YOU? 1961 - 1963

JOE E ROSS - OFFICER GUNTHER TOODY

FRED GWYNNE - OFFICER FRANCIS MULDOON

BEATRICE PONS - LUCILE TOODY

PAUL REED - CAPTAIN MARTIN BLOCK

ALBERT HENDERSON - OFFICER O'HARA

JOE WARREN - OFFICER STEINMETZ

AL LEWIS - OFFICER LEO SCHNAUSER

BRUCE KIRBY - OFFICER KISSEL

HANK GARRETT - OFFICER ED NICHOLSON

JIM GORMLEY - OFFICER NELSON

CHARLOTTE RAE - SILVIA SCHNAUSER

Centered in San Francisco's Haight-Ashbury district the Haight-Ashbury (nicknamed "The Hashbury") scene was anti-war, against capitalism and pro both love and dope.

JEFFERSON AIRPLANE

JIMI HENDRIX

On January 14, 1967, 20,000 hippies converged on San Francisco for the first "Human Be-In and Gathering of the Tribes" – an open-air event at the Polo Grounds in Golden Gate Park – it was the beginning of "The Summer of Love."

YOUR HEAD, YOU HAVE TO GO OUT OF YOUR MIND.

"TO LEARN HOW TO USE

TURN ON!

TUNE IN!

DROP OUT!

— TIMOTHY LEARY

Timothy Leary was an outspoken LSD advocate and attended numerous musical events and public forums that promoted the use of LSD in the mid-sixties. He coined the phrase "Turn On, Tune In, and Drop Out," and formed the "League of Spiritual Discovery," an LSD advocacy group.

QUICKSILVER MESSENGER SERVICE

MOBY GRAPE

THE GRATEFUL DEAD

BIG BROTHER & THE HOLDING COMPANY

HAIGHT

Ken Kesey's (pictured right) celebrated novel *One Flew Over the Cuckoo's Nest* was based on his experience in a government drug research program testing psychoactive drugs in 1959.

By the early 1960s, he and a group of individuals known as "The Merry Pranksters" openly used hallucinogenic drugs, wore outrageous attire, performed bizarre acts of street theater, and threw LSD parties known as "Acid Tests."

CREEDENCE CLEARWATER REVIVAL

"If you're going to San Francisco
Be sure to wear some flowers in your hair
If you're going to San Francisco
You're gonna meet some gentle people there

For those who come to San Francisco
Summertime will be a love-in there
In the streets of San Francisco
Gentle people with flowers in their hair

All across the nation such a strange vibration
People in motion
There's a whole generation with a new
 explanation
People in motion people in motion

For those who come to San Francisco
Be sure to wear some flowers in your hair
If you come to San Francisco
Summertime will be a love-in there

If you come to San Francisco
Summertime will be a love-in there."

"San Francisco," Scott McKenzie

"For a thousand days, she was the undisputed queen of a country that claims no royalty."

Jackie

MOON LANDING

9.32AM EDT, JULY 16, 1969 – APOLLO 11 LAUNCHES.
MISSION "TO PERFORM A MANNED LUNAR LANDING
AND RETURN."

4.18PM EDT, JULY 20, 1969 –

"Houston, Tranquility Base here.

10.55PM EDT, JULY 20, 1969 –
AN ESTIMATED 600 MILLION
PEOPLE IN 43 COUNTRIES
WATCH NEIL ARMSTRONG TAKE
HIS FIRST STEP ON THE MOON.

"That's one small
step for man,
one giant leap
for mankind."

CREW –
   NEIL A. ARMSTRONG
   MICHAEL COLLINS
   EDWIN E. "BUZZ" ALDRIN, JR.

12.15PM EDT, JULY 24,
1969 – APOLLO 11
SPLASHES DOWN IN
THE PACIFIC OCEAN.

TOTAL COST OF THE APOLLO SPACE PROGRAM, $25.4 BILLION

"My name is Bond, James Bond."

Dr. No - 1962

James Bond (Sean Connery)
Honey Ryder (Ursula Andress)
Sylvia Trench (Eunice Gayson)

Honey Ryder: *"Are you looking for shells too?"*
James Bond: *"No, I'm just looking."*

From Russia With Love - 1963

James Bond (Sean Connery)
Tatiana Romanova (Daniela Bianchi)
Rosa Klebb (Lotte Lenya)

James Bond: *"You're one of the most beautiful girls I've ever seen."*
Tatiana Romanova: *"I think my mouth is too big."*
James Bond: *"No it's the right size. For me, that is."*

Goldfinger - 1964

James Bond (Sean Connery)
Pussy Galore (Honor Blackman)
Jill Masterson (Shirley Eaton)
Tilly Masterson (Tania Mallet)

Pussy Galore: *"My name is Pussy Galore."*
James Bond: *"I must be dreaming!"*

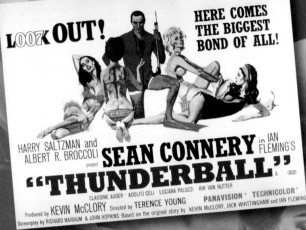

Thunderball - 1965

James Bond (Sean Connery)
Patricia Fearing (Mollie Peters)
Dominique "Domino" Derval (Claudine Auger)
Fiona Volpe (Luciana Paluzzi)

James Bond, to Domino:
"That's the first time I've tasted women. They're rather good."

You Only Live Twice - 1967

James Bond (Sean Connery)
Aki (Akiko Wakabayashi)
Kissy Suzuki (Mie Hama)
Helga Brandt (Karin Dor)

Aki, to James Bond: "I think I will enjoy very much serving under you."

On Her Majesty's Secret Service - 1969

James Bond (George Lazenby)
Comtessa Teresa "Tracy" di Vicenzo (Diana Rigg)

The look of swingin' london is all about: fashion miniskirts
catsuits, maxi vests, colored tights, pant suits
geometric patterns, arran sweaters, capes, pvc
sassoon, diana vreeland, the models shrimp, veruschka
the hairstyles five-point cut, the asymmetrical bob, the nancy

"England Swings!"

Roger Miller, 1965

everywhere miniskirts, hotpants, vinyl, go-go boots, fur vests, a-line, sleeveless tops, bell bottoms, deerstalker hats, where to go carnaby street, fashion superstars mary quant, vidal twiggy, penelope tree, david bailey, photographers richard avedon, kwan, the rolled florentine pageboy, liquid make-up eyeliner.

JOSEPH E. LEVINE PRESENTS A MIKE NICHOLS-LAWRENCE TURMAN PRODUCTION

This
is
Benjamin
He's
a little
worried
about
his
future

THE GRADUATE

ACADEMY AWARD
WINNER
BEST ACHIEVEMENT
IN DIRECTION
**MIKE
NICHOLS**

STARRING
ANNE BANCROFT AND DUSTIN HOFFMAN · KATHARINE ROSS

SCREENPLAY BY
CALDER WILLINGHAM AND BUCK HENRY

SONGS BY
PAUL SIMON

PERFORMED BY
SIMON AND GARFUNKEL

PRODUCED BY
LAWRENCE TURMAN

DIRECTED BY
MIKE NICHOLS

TECHNICOLOR® PANAVISION®

United Artists

"Mrs
Robinson,
you're trying
to seduce
me... aren't
you?"

The film cost
$3 million
to make but
grossed over
$100 million
and was
nominated
for 7
Academy
Awards®.

Starring:
Anne Bancroft as Mrs Robinson
Dustin Hoffman as Benjamin Braddock
Katharine Ross as Elaine Robinson
William Daniels as Mr Braddock
Murray Hamilton as Mr Robinson

offman

Dustin Hoffman's film debut was with a tiny role in the feature *The Tiger Makes Out* in 1967, followed by a similarly brief appearance in *Un Dollaro per Sette Vigliachi* later that same year.

It was in his highly acclaimed role in the theatrical farce *Eh?* that he was first spotted by director Mike Nichols, who cast him in the lead role of *The Graduate* which earned him an Oscar® nomination.

Starring:
Dustin Hoffman as
Enrico Salvatore "Ratso" Rizzo
Jon Voight as Joe Buck

Midnight Cowboy was the first mainstream movie to receive an X-rating and the only X-rated movie to win a Best Picture Oscar®.

The Beach Boys

Surfin'
Good Vibrations
Surfin' Safari
Surfin' USA
I Get Around
Help Me, Rhonda
California Girls
Barbara Ann
Fun, Fun, Fun

"Let's go *Surfing* now
Everybody's learning how
Come on and safari with me."

"Surfin' Safari" by The Beach Boys

Annette Funicello

Beach Party	1963
Muscle Beach Party	1964
Bikini Beach	1964
Pajama Party	1964
Beach Blanket Bingo	1965
How to Stuff a Wild Bikini	1965
The Ghost in the Invisible Bikini	1966

Jan and Dean

Surf City

Honolulu Lulu

Drag City

Dead Man's Curve

The Little Old Lady from Pasadena

"Coffee, tea

Braniff Airlines, 1966

or me?"

"I always feel like I'm sort of giving a party."

We've hired 15,873 stewardesses. Since 1933.
So let us tell you something about girls. Makeup can change a face, but it can't change a personality. A girl has to have that special attitude. If she does, you get that special service. If she doesn't, we both pay.
Sandy Norris is 22. She's from Weslaco, Texas. And after one year on the job, this is what she told us about being a stewardess.

"At first I was bashful.
But then people began thanking me for an enjoyable flight.
I liked that. And I realized how much I wanted everything to go just right.
That I had fun when they did."

We'll keep combing America for girls like Sandy. And as soon as we meet them, we promise to introduce them to you.
Girls who bring a little something extra to their job. That's the American Way.

**Fly the American Way.
American Airlines.**

American Airlines, 1968

PSA AISLE SEATS $13.50*

WHILE THEY LAST

On other airlines everybody wants the window seats. On PSA they prefer the aisle view. Guess why? More new jets and 900 flights a week connecting Northern and Southern California. Call PSA or your travel agent for something very interesting on the aisle.

*L.A.-San Francisco 727 Super Jets

PSA gives you a lift

PSA Airlines, 1968

Think of her as your mother.

She only wants what's best for you.
A cool drink. A good dinner. A soft pillow and a warm blanket.
This is not just maternal instinct. It's the result of the longest Stewardess training in the industry.
Training in service, not just a beauty course.
Service, after all, is what makes professional travellers prefer American.
And makes new travellers want to keep on flying with us.
So we see that every passenger gets the same professional treatment.
That's the American Way.

Fly the American Way
American Airlines

American Airlines, 1968

"The young ladies graduate with honors in the gracious art of making people happy."
American Airlines, 1960

BASKETBALL

1964-65, the NBA widened the foul lane from 12 to 16 feet in an effort to lessen the dominance of big men and keep the game open and moving.

The ABA, a second competing professional league, was established in the 1967-68 season with 11 teams playing a 78-game schedule.

NBA CHAMPIONSHIP

1959-60	Boston Celtics def. St. Louis Hawks	4-3
1960-61	Boston Celtics def. St. Louis Hawks	4-1
1961-62	Boston Celtics def. Los Angeles Lakers	4-3
1962-63	Boston Celtics def. Los Angeles Lakers	4-2
1963-64	Boston Celtics def. San Francisco Warriors	4-1
1964-65	Boston Celtics def. Los Angeles Lakers	4-1
1965-66	Boston Celtics def. Los Angeles Lakers	4-3
1966-67	Philadelphia 76ers def. San Francisco Warriors	4-2
1967-68	Boston Celtics def. Los Angeles Lakers	4-2
1968-69	Boston Celtics def. Los Angeles Lakers	4-3

The Boston Celtics dominated the 1960s, winning 9 and out 10 seasons.

"Wilt the Stilt" Chamberlain

Also known as "The Big Dipper," 7' 1" Wilt Chamberlain was drafted to the Philadelphia Warriors in 1959, winning the MVP award for the 1959-60 season as well as "Rookie of the Year." He led the NBA in scoring seven years in a row and is the only NBA player to score 4,000 points in a season. His dominance of the game also created many rule changes, from widening the lane, instituting offensive goal-tending and free-throw shooting.

Jerry West

During his 14-year playing career with the Los Angeles Lakers, West became synonymous with brilliant basketball. He was the third player in league history to reach 25,000 points (after Wilt Chamberlain and Oscar Robertson), was an All-Star every year of his career and led Los Angeles to the NBA Finals nine times. He left the game holding records for career postseason scoring and the highest average in a playoff series.

Oscar "The Big O" Robertson

At 6' 5" and 210 pounds, Robertson was the first "big guard." During his 14-year NBA career with the Cincinnati Royals and the Milwaukee Bucks, Robertson became the top-scoring guard of all time, amassing 26,710 points. He was NBA Rookie of the Year in 1960-61, played in 12 straight NBA All-Star Games, was selected to the All-NBA First Team nine consecutive seasons and won the NBA Most Valuable Player Award in 1963-64.

TODAY'S MODERN WOMAN

Pantsuits

Pantsuits, culottes, Bermuda shorts, Capri pants, cabin boy pants, cat suits.

1960	1961	1962	1963	1964

is wearing...

Smock-Frocks

A model wearing a paisley patterned A-line mini-dress.

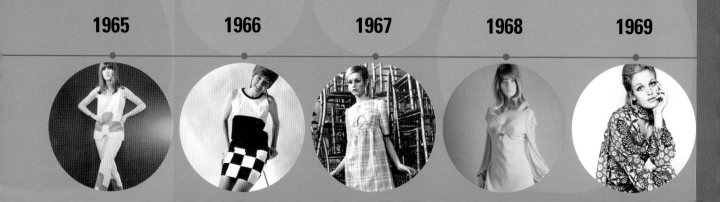

1965   **1966**   **1967**   **1968**   **1969**

THE CAST...

Adam West
Batman / Bruce Wayne

Burt Ward
Robin / Richard "Dick" Grayson

Alan Napier
Alfred

Neil Hamilton
Commissioner James Gordon

Stafford Repp
Chief O'Hara

Madge Blake
Aunt Harriet Cooper
(1966 – 1967)

Yvonne Craig
Batgirl / Barbara Gordon
(1967 – 1968)

William Dozier
Announcer and series creator

GASP!

"SAME BAT TIME, SAME BAT CHANNEL!"

GUEST VILLAINS...

Burgess Meredith
The Penguin

Frank Gorshin
The Riddler

Julie Newmar
Catwoman
(also played by Eartha Kitt
and Lee Meriwether)

Cesar Romero
The Joker

Liberace
Chandell

Vincent Price
Egghead

Milton Berle
Louis the Lilac

Ethel Merman
Lola Lasagne

Pierre Salinger
Lucky Pierre

Victor Buono
King Tut

George Sanders
Mr Freeze

Anne Baxter
Zelda

Roddy McDowell
The Bookworm

Art Carney
The Archer

Shelley Winters
Ma Parker

Cliff Robertson
Shame

Pow!

Sock!

Ka-Pow!

THE "BATCLIMB"

The "Batclimb" was a popular feature in the series, where guest stars would put their heads out of a window while Batman & Robin appeared to be walking up a building wall.

Lid

Bag

Stoned

Wasted

Toke

Bong

Reefer

High

Stash

Roach

"Everybody must get stoned."

"Rainy Day Woman," **Bob Dylan**

"I get high with a little help from my friends."

"With a Little Help from My Friends," **The Beatles**

"Jo Jo left his home in Tucson, Arizona,
for some California Grass."

"Get Back," **The Beatles**

frodis, ganja, grass, green, hashish, herb, indo, instaga, KB (kind bud/killer bud), kind, kipp, Mary Jane, mellow fellow, moss,

Bomb, bud, buddha, butters/utter-butters, chillsprout, chimichangas, chronic, crunkler, dagga, dak, dank, dee, dope,

nugget, pot, rope, scrazzlerb, shwag (low-quality marijuana), skunk, smoke, tampiko, weed, whacko-tobacco.

Cannabis: *pron. ka-na-bis*, *n*. Etymology: Latin, *hemp*, from Greek *kannabis*; akin to Old English *hænep* hemp: any of the preparations (*as marijuana or hashish*) or chemicals (*as THC*) that are derived from the hemp and are psychoactive.

Winner of five U.S. figure skating championships (1964 – 1968) and three world titles (1966 – 1968).

PEGGY FLEMING

"Queen of the Ice"

At the 1968 Winter Olympic Games in Grenoble, France, skating to Tchaikovsky's *Pathetique*, Peggy delivered a graceful, impeccable performance, finishing 88.2 points ahead of her nearest competitor and winning America's only gold medal of the Games.

The 5-foot-3, 109-pound Fleming started skating competitively when she was eleven.

"...a unique combination of athletic ability, technical control, great style, and immense musicality."

Dick Button,
2-time Olympic gold medallist
and 5-time World Champion.

The Brides of Dracula – 1960

What Ever Happened to Baby Jane? - 1962

The Haunting – 1963   Day of the Triffids - 1963

Children of the Damned - 1963   The Raven – 1963

Night of the   THE DAMNED - 1964
Living Dead - 1968

Pray
for
Rosemary's
Baby

Rosemary's Baby - 1968

The Time Machine – 1960

The Man With X-Ray Eyes – 1963

Fantastic Voyage – 1966

One Million Years B.C. – 1966

Who gives up the pill? Who takes sex to outer space? Who's the girl of the 21st century? Who nearly dies of pleasure?

Who seduces an angel?

BARBARELLA

Who's the bird in the gilded cage?

Who conveys love by hand?

Who strips in space?

The Doomsday Machine - 1967

2001: A SPACE ODYSSEY - 1968

Barbarella – 1968

"Take this down, Miss Jones."

"INCREDIBLE!
Now you can add,
subtract and multiply
electrically at home
or office."

Smith-Corona Figurematic, 1964

"COPIES
EVERYTHING
in any of 7
COLORS… plus
sparkling black
on white, too!"

Apeco Uni-Matic Copier, 1961

"Mail letters
over the
phone!"

Xerox Telecopier, 1966

"Here's a SMART way to
keep a GOOD secretary
HAPPIER – and LONGER."

Dictaphone, 1964

"Your secretary will
love its alive, eager
response. You'll
admire its styling
and high-volume
output."

IBM Electric Typewriter, 1960

"Double the action in
your office space…
such flexibility,
such completeness,
such comfort!"

Royal Office Furniture, 1961

THE RAT PACK

Frank Sinatra
Dean Martin
Sammy Davis, Jr.
Peter Lawford
Joey Bishop

"The Rat Pack" was born in 1959 when Frank Sinatra joined Dean Martin on stage at the Sands Hotel and Casino in Las Vegas. It would become a routine that would last for seven years.

"The Rat Pack" would perform at the Sands at night and, in between partying, would make films during the day.

"WE'RE NOT SETTING OUT TO MAKE HAMLET OR GONE WITH THE WIND. THE IDEA IS TO HANG OUT TOGETHER, FIND FUN WITH BROADS AND TO HAVE A GREAT TIME."
FRANK SINATRA

The name "Rat Pack" was coined when actress Lauren Bacall came across the gang as they were recovering from a five-day, non-stop rampage through Las Vegas. **"You look like a ...Rat Pack!"** she remarked.

The "Rat Pack's" first film, *Ocean's Eleven*, shot on location at the Sands Hotel and the Riviera Hotel and Casino, was released in 1960 and was followed by *Sergeant's Three* in 1962. By the last film, *Robin and the Seven Hoods*, released in 1964, Peter Lawford and Joey Bishop had dropped out of the cast and were replaced by Bing Crosby and Peter Falk.

FRANK SiNATRA · DEAN MARTiN · SAMMY DAViS, jr. IN
ROBiN AND THE 7 HOODS U

Co-Starring PETER FALK · BARBARA RUSH VICTOR BUONO and Bing CROSBY

Produced by FRANK SINATRA Directed by GORDON DOUGLAS Written by DAVID R. SCHWARTZ Executive Producer HOWARD W. KOCH A P-C PRODUCTION · TECHNICOLOR® PANAVISION® FROM WARNER BROS. as Allen A. Dale

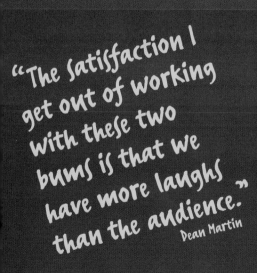

"The satisfaction I get out of working with these two bums is that we have more laughs than the audience."
Dean Martin

SIDNEY POITIER

"No one expected the son of a tomato farmer and a semi-literate lady to ever make a stir of any consequence."
SIDNEY POITIER

In 1963
Sidney Poitier
became the first African American to win an Oscar® for Best Actor.

In 1966
Poitier initiated the first Hollywood on-screen kiss
between a white person and a black person in
Guess Who's Coming to Dinner.

By 1968
he was the Number One
box-office star in the USA

"If you apply reason and logic to this career of mine, you're not going to get very far... So much of life, it seems to me, is determined by pure randomness."

SIDNEY POITIER

JIMI HENDRIX

James Marshal Hendrix, 1942-1970

After receiving an honorable discharge from the army in 1961, Jimi played guitar on numerous star tours including B.B. King, Sam Cooke, Soloman Burke, Chuck Jackson and Jackie Wilson, later joining Little Richard's band and going on to play with Ike and Tina Turner.

ERIC CLAPTON

While playing with The Bluesbreakers, Eric Clapton earned the nickname "Slowhand" as his forceful guitar playing often resulted in broken guitar strings, which he would then replace onstage while the crowd slow hand-clapped.

ALBUMS

The Yardbirds — Five Live Yardbirds (1964)
The Yardbirds — Sonny Boy Williamson & the Yardbirds (1965)
John Mayall with Eric Clapton — Bluesbreakers (1966)
Cream — Fresh Cream (1966)
Various Artists — What's Shakin' (1966)
Cream — Disraeli Gears (1967)
John Mayall's Bluesbreakers — Raw Blues (1967)
Cream — Wheels Of Fire (1968)
Blind Faith — Blind Faith (1969)
Plastic Ono Band — Live Peace in Toronto (1969)
Cream — Best Of Cream (1969)
Cream — Goodbye (1969)
Eric Clapton — Eric Clapton (1970)
Eric Clapton — The Best Of Eric Clapton (1970)
Derek & The Dominos — Layla And Other Assorted Love Songs (1970)
Delaney & Bonnie & Friends — On Tour with Eric Clapton (1970)
Cream — Live Cream (1970)
John Mayall's Bluesbreakers — Back to the Roots (1970)

BANDS

The Roosters — 1963
The Yardbirds — 1963-1965
John Mayall's Bluesbreakers — 1965-1966
Cream — 1966-1968
Blind Faith — 1969
Delaney & Bonnie & Friends — 1970
Derek & the Dominos — 1970

The Jimi Hendrix Experience, with Mitch Mitchell on drums and Noel Redding on bass, was formed in 1966 with former Animals bassist Chas Chandler. Jimi also had a side band, The Band of Gypsies – an all-black trio – who released one live album and played at Woodstock in 1969.

"Imagination is the key to my lyrics. The rest is painted with a little science fiction."

Jimi Hendrix

ALBUMS

Are You Experienced? **(1967)**

"Purple Haze"

"Hey Joe"

"The Wind Cries Mary"

"Are You Experienced?"

Axis: Bold as Love **(1968)**

"Spanish Castle Magic"

"Little Wing"

"Castles Made Of Sand"

"If 6 Was 9"

Electric Ladyland **(1968)**

"Voodoo Child (Slight Return)"

"Crosstown Traffic"

"Gypsy Eyes"

"All Along the Watchtower"

Smash Hits **(1969)**

"Red House"

"Stone Free"

Band of Gypsys **(1970)**

The Cry of Love **(1971)**

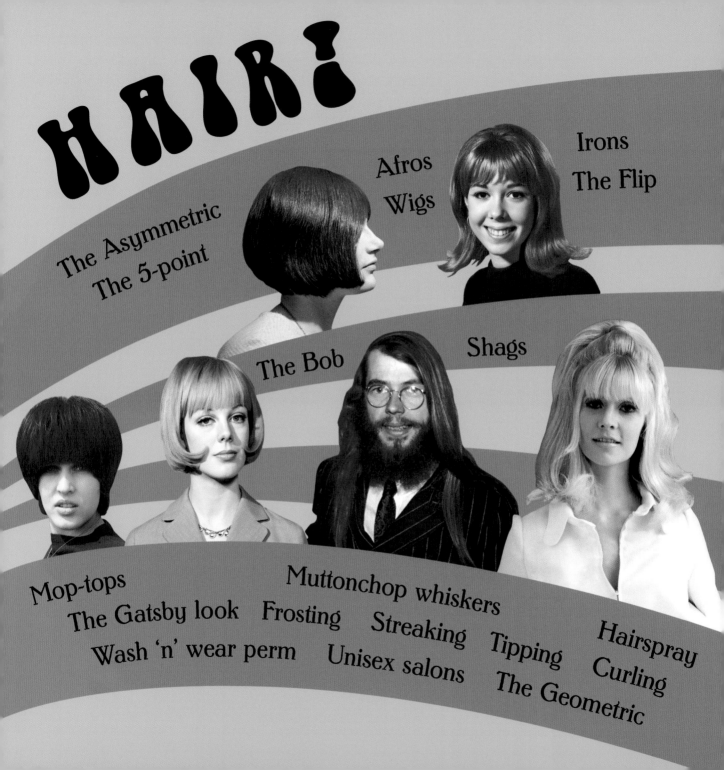

HAIR!

The Asymmetric
The 5-point

Afros
Wigs

Irons
The Flip

The Bob

Shags

Mop-tops

Muttonchop whiskers

The Gatsby look   Frosting   Streaking   Tipping   Hairspray   Curling

Wash 'n' wear perm   Unisex salons   The Geometric

"Hair: The American Tribal Love-Rock Musical"

Hair first opened at the Shakespeare Festival Public Theater in New York on October 17, 1967. It re-opened on Broadway at the Biltmore Theater on April 29, 1968 and in London's West End at the Shaftesbury Theatre, September 27, 1968.

Marsha Hunt became a star of the Broadway production of Hair.

"Gimme a head with hair, long beautiful hair Shining, gleaming, streaming, flaxen, waxen..."

"Hair," The Cowsills, 1968

SPORTS CAR STYLE!

Aston Martin DB5

1965 MGB GT

1967 E-Type Jaguar

1962 Triumph Spitfire

1965 Sunbeam Tiger

BRITAIN

1964 Ford Mustang

1963 Chevrolet Corvette Stingray

1967 Chevrolet Camaro

1962 Ford Thunderbird

"When I'm behind the wheel
Horses of gas and steel
The highway is my home
In fiberglass and chrome
Fantasy car shiny Corvette
Let's take a ride you can't forget
Come on pretty lady ride with me.

In my car
I'm captain of my destiny
In my car
Pretty babe come cruise with me."

"In My Car," The Beach Boys

1965 Pontiac GTO Convertible

FEMI

1961
Eleanor Roosevelt chairs President Kennedy's *The President's Commission on the Status of Women.*

1962
Helen Gurley Brown publishes *Sex and the Single Girl.*

1963
The Equal Pay Act is passed by Congress, promising equitable wages for the same work, regardless of the race, color, religion, national origin or sex of the worker.

Betty Friedan publishes *The Feminine Mystique.*

Gloria Steinem (pictured) writes *I Was a Playboy Bunny,* an article which recounts her experience as a waitress at Hugh Hefner's Playboy Club.

Yale Law School gives its first tenure to a woman, Ellen Ash Peters.

1964
Title VII of the Civil Rights Act is passed including a prohibition against employment discrimination on the basis of race, color, religion, national origin, or sex.

1965
Weeks v. Southern Bell marks a major triumph in the fight against restrictive labor laws and company regulations on the hours and conditions of women's work, which opens many previously male-only jobs to women.

Helen Gurley Brown becomes editor-in-chief of *Cosmopolitan* magazine.

"A liberated woman is one who has

1967
Muriel Siebert becomes the first woman to own a seat on the New York Stock Exchange.

1968
Executive Order 11246 prohibits sex discrimination by government contractors and requires affirmative action plans for hiring women.

The first female teacher is allowed to teach while visibly pregnant in Clear Creek School District, California.

1969
In Bowe v. Colgate-Palmolive Company, the Seventh Circuit Court of Appeals rules that women meeting the physical requirements can work in many jobs that had been for men only.

California adopts the nation's first "no fault" divorce law, allowing divorce by mutual consent.

1966
Betty Friedan (pictured), Gloria Steinem, Pauli Murray and other delegates of the Third National Conference of the Commission on the Status of Women, found the National Organization for Women which coins the phrases "Women's Lib" and the "glass ceiling."

sex before marriage and a job after."
Gloria Steinem

"The Colors" were used in campaigns on banners, pamphlets, newspapers, posters, and predominantly in clothing such as scarves, ribbons and jewelry.

It's Not Unusual
February 1965

Once Upon A Time
May 1965

With These Hands
July 1965

What's New Pussycat?
August 1965

Thunderball
January 1966

**Once There Was A Time
/ Not Responsible**
May 1966

This And That
August 1966

**Green Green Grass
Of Home**
November 1966

Detroit City
February 1967

**Funny Familiar
Forgotten Feelings**
April 1967

**I'll Never Fall
In Love Again**
July 1967

I'm Coming Home
November 1967

Delilah
February 1968

Help Yourself
July 1968

A Minute Of Your Time
November 1968

Love Me Tonight
May 1969

Without Love
December 1969

Tom Jones

Born Thomas Jones Woodward, Tom Jones began singing professionally in 1963, performing as "Tommy Scott and the Senators," a Welsh beat group.

"WHAT'S NEW PUSSYCAT?"

"I never thought I'd land in pictures with a face like mine." AUDREY HEPBURN

"She sparkles and glows with the fire of a finely cut diamond." *TIME* MAGAZINE

One Wild Oat 1951
Young Wives' Tales 1951
The Lavender Hill Mob 1951
Nous Irons A Monte-Carlo 1952
Roman Holiday 1953
Sabrina 1954
War and Peace 1956
Funny Face 1957
Love In The Afternoon 1957
The Nun's Story 1959
Green Mansions 1959
The Unforgiven 1960

Breakfast at Tiffany's 1961

The Children's Hour 1961
Charade 1963
Paris When It Sizzles 1964
My Fair Lady 1964
How To Steal A Million 1966
Wait Until Dark 1967
Two For the Road 1967

INTRODUCING:

GI Joe®

Super Ball

Etch-A-Sketch®

Skate Boards

The Game of Life®

Easy-Bake® Ovens

Twister®

Slot Cars

Sea Monkeys®

Black Light

Troll Dolls

Silly String

"Y'all come back now, y'hear?"

Buddy Ebsen –
Jed Clampett

Irene Ryan –
Granny Daisy May Moses

Donna Douglas –
Elly May Clampett

Max Bayer, Jr. –
Jethro Bodine

Raymond Bailey –
Milburn Drysdale

Nancy Kulp –
Miss Jane Hathaway

Harriet E. MacGibbon –
Mrs. Margaret Drysdale
(1962 – 1969)

Bea Benaderet –
Cousin Pearl Bodine
(1962 – 1963)

"Come and listen to a story 'bout a man named Jed

A poor mountaineer, barely kept his family fed

Then one day he was shootin' at some food

And up through the ground came a bubblin' crude

Oil that is, black gold, Texas Tea

Well the first thing you know ole Jed's a millionaire,

Kinfolk said 'Jed move away from there'

Said 'Californy is the place you ought to be'

So they loaded up the truck and moved to Beverly

Hills, that is. Swimmin' pools, movie stars."

The Beverly
HILLBILLIES

1962 – 1971

"SKIIIPPERRRR!!!"

Bob Denver –
Gilligan

Alan Hale Jr. –
Skipper Jonas Grumby

Jim Backus –
Thurston Howell III

Natalie Schafer –
Eunice Wentworth
"Lovey" Howell

Tina Louise –
Ginger Grant

Dawn Wells –
Mary Ann Summers

Russell Johnson –
Roy "The Professor"
Hinkley, Jr. Ph.D.

"Just sit right back and you'll
   hear a tale
A tale of a fateful trip
That started from this tropic port
Aboard this tiny ship

The mate was a mighty sailing man
The skipper brave and sure
Five passengers set sail that day
For a three hour tour, a three
   hour tour

The weather started getting rough
The tiny ship was tossed
If not for the courage of
   the fearless crew
The Minnow would be lost,
   the Minnow would be lost

The ship set ground on the shore
   of this uncharted desert isle
With Gilligan, the Skipper too,
   the millionaire and his wife
The movie star, the professor
   and Mary Ann
Here on Gilligan's isle."

Gilligan's Island 1964 – 1967

"Future homes will be able to face in any direction - turned at will by your electricity."

America's Independent Electric Light and Power Companies, 1965

Bell Telephone Systems, 1963

Motorola, 1963

"The future is now."

RCA Victor, 1969

BONNIE AND

Warren Beatty's film debut was in Elia Kazan's *Splendor in the Grass* (1961), co-starring Natalie Wood. *Bonnie and Clyde* however was his breakthrough film which he also produced.

Clyde was the leader, Bonnie wrote po...

C.W., was a Myrna Loy fan who had a bluish...
told corny jokes and carried a Kodak. B...
who kept her fingers in her ears duri...
checkers and photographed each other in...
listened to Eddie Cantor on the radio,

They were the strangest damned gang...

WARREN
FAYE DU

BONNIE

MICHAEL J. POLLARD · GEN...

DAVID NEWMAN and ROBERT BENTON

TECHNICOLOR® FROM WARN...

Notorious for his many off-screen romances, he was romantically linked with many of his leading ladies, including Natalie Wood, Joan Collins, Julie Christie and Elizabeth Taylor, and was co-respondent in Leslie Caron's 1966 divorce case.

CLYDE

1967

Bonnie and Clyde was nominated for ten Academy Awards® (winning two – for Best Supporting Actress and Best Cinematography) and was one of Warner Bros.' top-grossing movies of the decade, along with *My Fair Lady*.

& Faye Dunaway as Bonnie Parker

Faye Dunaway was catapulted into the spotlight with *Bonnie and Clyde* and within a year of its release had made the covers of *Newsweek, Look* and *Life* magazines. She followed *Bonnie and Clyde* starring opposite Steve McQueen in *The Thomas Crown Affair* in 1968.

Her role in *Bonnie and Clyde* influenced international fashions and her beret and blonde hairstyle sparked a retro-'30s look that made midi-skirts and maxi-skirts fashion essentials in the late 1960s.

"Over and Over"

"I'm Telling You Now"

"Doo wah diddy diddy"

"Mrs Brown You've Got a Lovely Daughter"

"To Sir with Love"

"House of the Rising Sun"

"Wild Thing"

"Honky Tonk Woman"

"Ruby Tuesday"

"Paint it Black"

"Get Off My Cloud"

"I'm Henry VIII I Am"

"I Can't Get No Satisfaction"

The Who

The Yardbirds

The Dave Clark Five   The Hollies   Manfred Mann   The Small Faces

Herman's Hermits   Lulu

Freddie and the Dreamers   Gerry and the Pacemakers   The Animals

The Troggs   The Kinks

The Moody Blues   The Rolling Stones

THE BRITISH INVASION

HOW LOW CAN

In 1963 Chubby Checker released a song called "Limbo Rock" which quickly soared to Number One on the charts, becoming the top song of the year.

"Every limbo boy and girl
All around the limbo world
Gonna do the limbo rock
All around the limbo clock
Jack be limbo, Jack be quick
Jack go unda limbo stick
All around the limbo clock
Hey, let's do the limbo rock

Limbo lower now
Limbo lower now
How low can you go

First you spread your limbo feet
Then you move to limbo beat
Limbo ankolimboneee,
Bend back like a limbo tree
Jack be limbo, Jack be quick
Jack go unda limbo stick
All around the limbo clock
Hey, let's do the limbo rock

Get yourself a limbo girl
Give that chick a limbo whirl
There's a limbo moon above
You will fall in limbo love
Jack be limbo, Jack be quick
Jack go unda limbo stick
All around the limbo clock
Hey, let's do the limbo rock

Don't move that limbo bar
You'll be a limbo star
How low can you go."

"Limbo Rock," Chubby Checker

YOU GO?

Originating in Trinidad, the Limbo was actually part of a funeral dance. The act was meant to symbolize the passage that the soul of the departed would take between life and the afterlife. Being able to pass under the bar without disturbing the pole or falling down was difficult – symbolizing the difficulty of the journey to heaven.

The Limbo was showcased in the 1960 movie *Where the Boys Are* and for the next year and a half it spread like wildfire.

American tourists demonstrated the limbo for friends back home. Boscoe Holder, a dancer from Trinidad, was one of the most famous limbo artists and used it in his dance routine. As more people were exposed to it, the limbo craze took off, first among teenagers and beatniks, then among their parents at dinner parties.

Dick Van Dyke Show
1961 – 1966

"Ohhh, Robbbb!"

Cast

Dick Van Dyke
Robert 'Rob' Petrie

Mary Tyler Moore
Laura Petrie

Rose Marie
Sally Rogers

Morey Amsterdam
Maurice 'Buddy' Sorrell

Richard Deacon
Melvin 'Mel' Cooley

Larry Mathews
Richard Rosebud 'Ritchie/Rich' Petrie

Carl Reiner
Alan Brady (1963-1966)

Herb Vigran
Alfred Reinbeck

Ann Morgan Guilbert
Millie Helper

Jerry Paris
Jerry Helper

"So you think that you've got trouble, well, trouble's a bubble
So tell ol' Mr Trouble to get lost
Why not hold your head up high and stop cryin', start tryin'
And don't forget to keep your fingers crossed
When you find the joy of livin' is lovin' and givin'
You'll be there when the winning dice are tossed
A smile is just a frown that's turned upside down
So smile and that frown'll defrost
And don't forget to keep your fingers crossed."

Andy Griffith Show
1960 – 1968

Cast

Andy Griffith
Sheriff Andy Taylor
(1960-1968)

Don Knotts
Deputy Barney Fife
(1960-1965)

Frances Bavier
Aunt Bee Taylor (1960-1970)

Ron Howard
Opie Taylor

Jack Dodson
Howard Sprague (1966-68)

Jim Nabors
Gomer Pyle (1963-64)

George Lindsey
Goober Pyle (1965-1968)

Elinor Donahue
Ellie Walker (1960-61)

Clint Howard
Leon

"Well, now, take down your fishin' pole and meet me at The Fishin' Hole
We may not get a bite all day, but don't you rush away

What a great place to rest your bones and mighty fine for skippin' stones
You'll feel fresh as a lemonade, a-settin' in the shade

Whether it's hot
whether it's cool
oh what a spot
for whistlin' like a fool..."

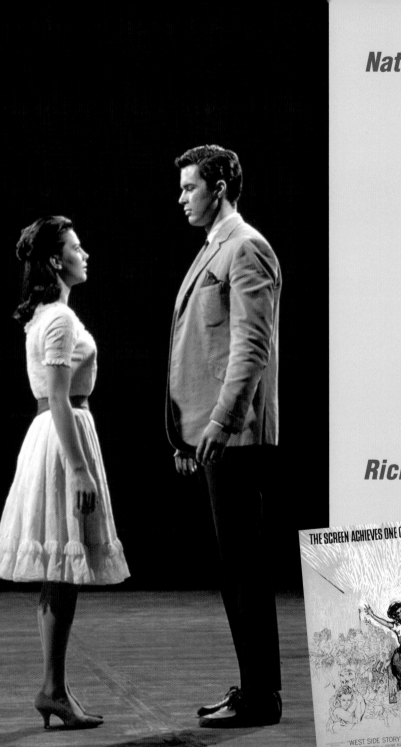

Natalie Wood as **Maria**

Jet Song

Something's Coming

Maria

America

Cool

One Hand, One Heart

Tonight

I Feel Pretty

Somewhere

Procession and Nightmare

Gee, Officer Krupke

A Boy Like That/I Have a Love

Richard Beymer as **Tony**

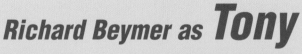

THE SCREEN ACHIEVES ONE OF THE GREAT ENTERTAINMENTS IN THE HISTORY OF MOTION PICTURES

WEST SIDE STORY

NATALIE WOOD   RICHARD BEYMER   RUSS TAMBLYN   RITA MORENO   GEORGE CHAKIRIS

"I like to be in America!
O.K. by me in America!
Ev'rything free in America
For a small fee in America!"
AMERICA

WEST SIDE STORY, 1961

Winner of 10 Academy Awards® including:
Best Picture, Best Director, Best Supporting Actor,
Best Supporting Actress and Best Music

THE JETS

Ice, Action, A-Rab, Baby John, Snowboy, Tiger, Joyboy, Big Deal. Mouth Piece, Gee-Tar & their girls Graziella, Velma and Anybodys

& THE SHARKS

Tony, Chino, Pepe, Indio, Juano, Loco, Rocco, Luis,Toro, Del Campo, Chile & their girls Consuelo, Rosalia and Francisca

THE DOORS

THE DOORS WERE FORMED IN LOS ANGELES IN 1965 BY UCLA FILM STUDENTS RAY MANZAREK (KEYBOARDS) AND JIM MORRISON (VOCALS) WITH GUITARIST ROBBY KRIEGER AND DRUMMER JOHN DENSMORE.

THE GROUP SIGNED TO ELEKTRA RECORDS IN 1966 AND RELEASED THEIR FIRST ALBUM, *THE DOORS*, FEATURING THE HIT "LIGHT MY FIRE" IN 1967. WITH THEIR UNIQUE BLEND OF BLUES, CLASSICAL, EASTERN AND POP MUSIC AND MORRISON'S HIGHLY POETIC LYRICS, THE BAND SOUNDED LIKE NO OTHER AND THEIR DEBUT ALBUM WAS A MASSIVE HIT.

ALBUMS

1967
STRANGE DAYS

1967
THE DOORS

1968
WAITING FOR THE SUN

1969
THE SOFT PARADE

SINGLES

1967
LIGHT MY FIRE

1967
PEOPLE ARE STRANGE

1968
HELLO, I LOVE YOU

1968
LOVE ME TWO TIMES

1968
THE UNKNOWN SOLDIER

"THERE ARE THINGS KNOWN, AND THERE ARE THINGS UNKNOWN, AND IN BETWEEN ARE THE DOORS."

JIM MORRISON

"IF MY POETRY AIMS TO ACHIEVE ANYTHING,

IT'S TO DELIVER PEOPLE FROM THE LIMITED WAYS

IN WHICH THEY SEE AND FEEL."

JIM MORRISON

5...4...3...2...1...0...

THUNDERBIRDS

by Gerry Anderson

Calling International Rescue!

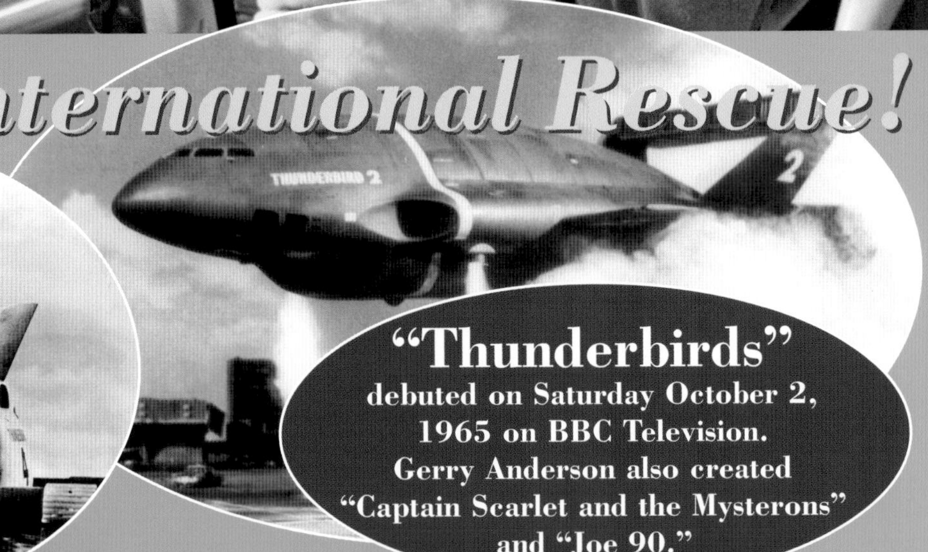

THUNDERBIRD 2

THUNDERBIRD 4

"**Thunderbirds**"
debuted on Saturday October 2,
1965 on BBC Television.
Gerry Anderson also created
"Captain Scarlet and the Mysterons"
and "Joe 90."

Secret Agent

Pilot Thunderbird 2

Pilot Thunderbird 1

Pilot Thunderbird 3

Lady Penelope Creighton Ward

Virgil Tracy

Scott Tracy

Alan Tracy

Pilot Thunderbird 4

Gordon Tracy

Brains

Jeff Tracy

Tin-tin

Scientific Assistant

Scientist

John Tracy

Head of International Rescue

Space Monitor Thunderbird 5

F.A.B.1: **Top Speed 200 miles per hour. Piloted by Parker with Lady Penelope. Specialized Equipment: Radiator-mounted cannon, twin sniper-sighted machine guns, rear-mounted harpoons, smoke-screen generator, cannons and hydrofoil.**

Drink a can of Metrecal®* and you've had the nutrition of steak, potatoes, peas and carrots. But not the calories. Metrecal has only 225.

(And it comes in 14 different flavors—every one right out of an ice cream parlor.)

Metrecal for lunch and some common sense at other meals will help keep your weight right where you want it.

Two Metrecal meals a day (lunch and dinner), and you can lose weight steadily.

As for 3 a day, talk it over with your doctor first. You might disappear.

The Metrecal steak.

About this picture: Our photographer said,"Since Metrecal's a complete meal, let's shoot it like one."

Metrecal, 1969

Diet Imperial, 1967

Rice Council of America, 1967

Grape-Nuts, 1968

Slender, 1969

Weight Watchers began in **1961** when a 214-pound housewife from Queens, **Jean Nidetch,** found a diet she could live with, and lost 72 pounds. Wanting to share her success with others, she invited six overweight friends over to support one another in their weight loss aims.

Weight Watchers was incorporated in May **1963** and the first public meeting was held in a loft in Queens. 400 people turned up to the first (unadvertised) meeting.

DIET is a four-letter word

Barbra Streisand

Shirley Bassey

"I am simple, complex, generous, selfish, unattractive, beautiful, lazy, and driven."

"I'd like to think I represent glamour on stage. To me that's what this business is all about."

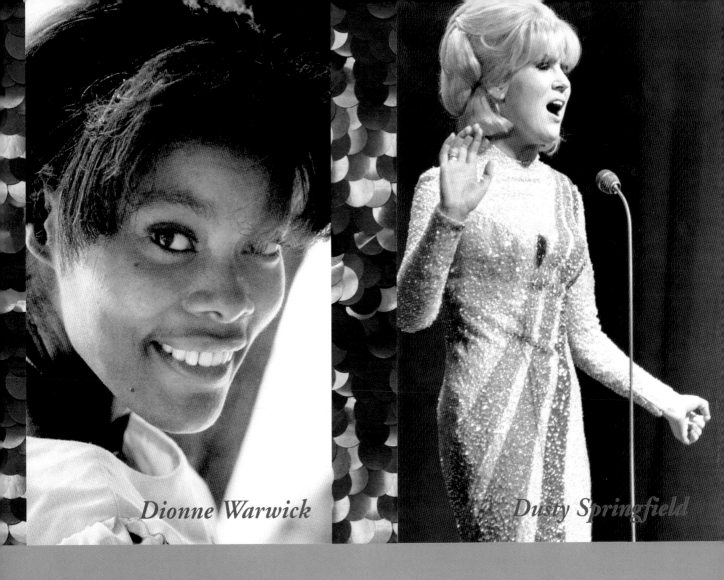

Dionne Warwick

Dusty Springfield

"I'm the little girl who brought downtown uptown."

"It's marvellous to be popular, but foolish to think it will last."

Bob Gibson – St. Louis Cardinals 1959-1975. The ex-Harlem Globetrotter posted World Series records of seven consecutive wins and 17 strikeouts in a game, was Most Valuable Player in 1968, CY Young Award winner in 1968 and 1970, and won 9 Golden Glove Awards.

Louis Clark "Lou" Brock – Chicago Cubs 1961-1964, St. Louis Cardinals 1964-1979. Lou Brock's 938 stolen bases set an all-time high. He also collected 3,000 hits and hit 149 career roundtrippers, including a 500-foot blast that landed in the Polo Grounds' center field bleachers in 1962.

Brooks Robinson – Baltimore Orioles 1955-1977. Known as "The Human Vacuum Cleaner," Brooks Robinson hit 268 career home runs. He earned the league's MVP Award in 1964 and the World Series MVP in 1970.

World Series

1960 – Pittsburgh Pirates def. New York Yankees **4-3**

1961 – New York Yankees def. Cincinnati Reds **4-1**

1962 – New York Yankees def. San Francisco Giants **4-3**

1963 – Los Angeles Dodgers def. New York Yankees **4-0**

1964 – St. Louis Cardinals def. New York Yankees **4-3**

1965 – Los Angeles Dodgers def. Minnesota Twins **4-3**

1966 – Baltimore Orioles def. Los Angeles Dodgers **4-0**

1967 – St. Louis Cardinals def. Boston Red Sox **4-3**

1968 – Detroit Tigers def. St. Louis Cardinals **4-3**

1969 – New York Mets def. Baltimore Orioles **4-1**

"Mr Tiger" Al Kaline – Detroit Tigers 1953-1974. Over 22 seasons he accumulated 3,007 hits, 399 home runs, Golden Gloves and 15 All-Star team selections.

"Hammerin'" Hank Aaron – Milwaukee Braves, Atlanta Braves, Milwaukee Brewers 1954-1976. Earned his nickname by hitting 755 home runs in his career. Won three Golden Glove awards, earned National League Most Valuable Player honors in 1957, and appeared in a record 24 All-Star Games. When he retired he ranked first in home runs, games played, total bases, runs batted in and times at bat, was second in number of hits and tied with Babe Ruth in runs scored.

Juan Marichal – San Francisco Giants 1960-1973. Known as the "Dominican Dandy" he had 6 20-win seasons, a no-hitter against Houston in 1963 and was named to 9 All-Star teams.

Harmon "Killer" Killebrew – Washington Senators 1955-1960, Minnesota Twins 1961-1974. His 573 career roundtrippers rank fifth on the all-time list and second only to Babe Ruth in the American League. He won the American League MVP Award in 1969.

Roberto Clemente – Pittsburgh Pirates 1955-1972. A member of the exclusive 3,000-Hit Club, he led the national league in batting four times and earned National League MVP honors in 1966.

1968 World Series

In a game billed as one of the greatest of the World Series, the Detroit Tigers came back from a 3-1 deficit to defeat the defending champion St. Louis Cardinals in seven games. Mickey Lolich received accolades for winning three games for Detroit that gave the Tigers their first championship crown since 1945.

Sanford "Sandy" Koufax – Los Angeles Dodgers 1958-1966. Set an all-time record with 4 no-hitters in 4 consecutive seasons capped by a perfect game in 1965. Voted Most Valuable Player in 1963 and CY Young Award Winner 1963, 1965 and 1966.

Frank Robinson – Cincinnati Reds, Baltimore Orioles, Los Angeles Dodgers, California Angels, Cleveland Indians 1956-1976. He was the first to be chosen Most Valuable Player in both leagues – the National League in 1961 and the American League in 1966. He ranks fourth on the all-time home run list with 586, trailing only Hank Aaron, Babe Ruth and Willie Mays.

"Hey, hey, We're the Monkees!"

Mike Nesmith

Davy Jones

Mickey Dolenz

Peter Tork

Albums
1966 The Monkees
1967 More of the Monkees
1967 Headquarters
1967 Pisces, Aquarius, Capricorn & Jones Ltd.
1968 The Birds, the Bees and the Monkees
1968 Head
1969 Instant Replay
1969 The Monkees Present

Top 10 Singles
1966 Last Train to Clarksville
1966 I'm a Believer
1967 A Little Bit Me, A Little Bit You
1967 Pleasant Valley Sunday
1967 Daydream Believer
1968 Valleri

"The Monkees" television show premiered on NBC in September 1966 and ran for 58 shows, finishing on August 19, 1968.

"I think you're the greatest comic talent since the Marx Brothers. **I've never missed one of your programs.**"

John Lennon to Mike Nesmith

1962

COLUMBIA PICTURES presents THE SAM SPIEGEL · DAVID LEAN Production of

LAWRENCE OF ARABIA

WINNER OF 7 ACADEMY AWARDS
INCLUDING
BEST PICTURE
OF THE YEAR

ALEC GUINNESS · ANTHONY QUINN · JACK HAWKINS · JOSE FERRER
ANTHONY QUAYLE · CLAUDE RAINS · ARTHUR KENNEDY
and PETER O'TOOLE as 'LAWRENCE'
with OMAR SHARIF as 'ALI' introducing PETER O'TOOLE as 'LAWRENCE'

SCREENPLAY BY ROBERT BOLT · PRODUCED BY SAM SPIEGEL · DIRECTED BY DAVID LEAN

A HORIZON BRITISH PRODUCTION IN TECHNICOLOR

Peter O'Toole – T.E. Lawrence

Alec Guinness – Prince Feisal

Anthony Quinn – Auda abu Tayi

Jack Hawkins – General Allenby

Omar Sharif – Sherif Ali ibn el Kharish

José Ferrer – Turkish Bey (as José Ferrer)

Anthony Quayle – Colonel Harry Brighton

Claude Rains – Mr. Dryden

Arthur Kennedy – Jackson Bentley

Donald Wolfit – General Murray

In *Lawrence of Arabia*, which was filmed in Super Panavision 70mm scope, almost all movement goes from left to right. Director David Lean said he did this to emphasize that the film was a journey.

"*He was the most extraordinary man I ever knew.*"

Colonel Harry Brighton (Anthony Quayle) on Lawrence

Nominated for
10 Oscars®
(winning 7),
5 BAFTAs
(winning 4),
6 Golden Globes
(winning 5)
and a Grammy.

The film took almost 18 months to make
and was shot between May 1961 and
October 1962 in 11 different
locations including Spain,
Morocco, Jordan,
Wales and
England.

The nearly four-hour long film
has no female speaking roles.

While filming, Peter O'Toole referred to co-star Omar Sharif
as "Fred" stating that "no one in the world is called
Omar Sharif, your name must be Fred."

"Go Girl,

Go-go boots were popularized by Nancy Sinatra's song, "These Boots Are Made for Walkin'." The first go-go boot, a white, flat-heeled design, was created by designer Andres Courreges.

Go!"

Go-go dancers danced in clubs on platforms, pedestals and in cages, which were usually suspended above the crowd. They danced from 10pm to 2am, rotating with other girls and were usually paid $20 a night.

The Whiskey-a-Go-Go, arguably the world's first discotheque, opened in Hollywood on January 11, 1964.

"These boots are made for walking, and that's just what they'll do. One of these days these boots are gonna walk all over you."

"Are you ready, boots? Start walkin'."
Nancy Sinatra

Robert
Francis
"Bobby"
Kennedy

1925 – 1968

Attorney General
of the United States
1961-1964

United States Senator
1964-1968

Assassinated June 5, 1968,
Ambassador Hotel,
Los Angeles, California.

"All great questions must be raised by great voices, and the greatest voice is the voice of the people – speaking out – in prose, or painting or poetry or music; speaking out – in homes and halls, streets and farms, courts and cafes – let that voice speak and the stillness you hear will be the gratitude of mankind."

Address, New York City, January 22, 1963

> " I write fiction and I'm told it's autobiography, I write autobiography and I'm told it's fiction, so since I'm so dim and they're so smart, let them decide what it is or it isn't. "
>
> Philip Roth

1960

1. Advise and Consent, Allen Drury
2. Hawaii, James A. Michener
3. The Leopard, Giuseppe di Lampedusa
4. The Chapman Report, Irving Wallace
5. Ourselves to Know, John O'Hara
6. The Constant Image, Marcia Davenport
7. The Lovely Ambition, Mary Ellen Chase
8. The Listener, Taylor Caldwell
9. Trustee from the Toolroom, Nevil Shute
10. Sermons and Soda-Water, John O'Hara

1961

1. The Agony and the Ecstasy, Irving Stone
2. Franny and Zooey, J. D. Salinger
3. To Kill a Mockingbird, Harper Lee
4. Mila 18, Leon Uris
5. The Carpetbaggers, Harold Robbins
6. Tropic of Cancer, Henry Miller
7. Winnie Ille Pu, Alexander Lenard, trans.
8. Daughter of Silence, Morris West
9. The Edge of Sadness, Edwin O'Connor
10. The Winter of Our Discontent,
    John Steinbeck

1962

1. Ship of Fools, Katherine Anne Porter
2. Dearly Beloved, Anne Morrow Lindbergh
3. A Shade of Difference, Allen Drury
4. Youngblood Hawke, Herman Wouk
5. Franny and Zooey, J. D. Salinger
6. Fail-Safe, Eugene Burdick
    and Harvey Wheeler
7. Seven Days in May, Fletcher Knebel
    and Charles W. Bailey II
8. The Prize, Irving Wallace
9. The Agony and the Ecstasy, Irving Stone
10. The Reivers, William Faulkner

1963

1. The Shoes of the Fisherman, Morris West
2. The Group, Mary McCarthy
3. Raise High the Roof Beam, Carpenters, and
    Seymour – An Introduction, J. D. Salinger
4. Caravans, James A. Michener
5. Elizabeth Appleton, John O'Hara
6. Grandmother and the Priests, Taylor Caldwell
7. City of Night, John Rechy
8. The Glass-Blowers, Daphne du Maurier
9. The Sand Pebbles, Richard McKenna
10. The Battle of the Villa Fiorita,
    Rumer Godden

1964

1. The Spy Who Came in from the Cold,
    John Le Carré
2. Candy, Terry Southern and Mason Hoffenberg
3. Herzog, Saul Bellow
4. Armageddon, Leon Uris
5. The Man, Irving Wallace
6. The Rector of Justin, Louis Auchincloss
7. The Martyred, Richard E. Kim
8. You Only Live Twice, Ian Fleming
9. This Rough Magic, Mary Stewart
10. Convention, Fletcher Knebel
    and Charles W. Bailey II

1965

1. The Source, James A. Michener
2. Up the Down Staircase, Bel Kaufman
3. Herzog, Saul Bellow
4. The Looking Glass War, John Le Carré
5. The Green Berets, Robin Moore
6. Those Who Love, Irving Stone
7. The Man with the Golden Gun, Ian Fleming
8. Hotel, Arthur Hailey
9. The Ambassador, Morris West
10. Don't Stop the Carnival, Herman Wouk

1966

1. Valley of the Dolls, Jacqueline Susann
2. The Adventurers, Harold Robbins
3. The Secret of Santa Vittoria, Robert Crichton
4. Capable of Honor, Allen Drury
5. The Double Image, Helen MacInnes
6. The Fixer, Bernard Malamud
7. Tell No Man, Adela Rogers St. Johns
8. Tai-Pan, James Clavell
9. The Embezzler, Louis Auchincloss
10. All in the Family, Edwin O'Connor

1967

1. The Arrangement, Elia Kazan
2. The Confessions of Nat Turner,
    William Styron (tie)
2. The Chosen, Chaim Potok (tie)
4. Topaz, Leon Uris
5. Christy, Catherine Marshall
6. The Eighth Day, Thornton Wilder
7. Rosemary's Baby, Ira Levin
8. The Plot, Irving Wallace
9. The Gabriel Hounds, Mary Stewart
10. The Exhibitionist, Henry Sutton

1968

1. Airport, Arthur Hailey
2. Couples, John Updike
3. The Salzburg Connection, Helen MacInnes
4. A Small Town in Germany, John Le Carré
5. Testimony of Two Men, Taylor Caldwell
6. Preserve and Protect, Allen Drury
7. Myra Breckinridge, Gore Vidal
8. Vanished, Fletcher Knebel
9. Christy, Catherine Marshall
10. The Tower of Babel, Morris West

1969

1. Portnoy's Complaint, Philip Roth
2. The Godfather, Mario Puzo
3. The Love Machine, Jacqueline Susann
4. The Inheritors, Harold Robbins
5. The Andromeda Strain, Michael Crichton
6. The Seven Minutes, Irving Wallace
7. Naked Came the Stranger, Penelope Ashe
8. The Promise, Chaim Potok
9. The Pretenders, Gwen Davis
10. The House on the Strand,
    Daphne du Maurier

Jacqueline Susann

Valley of the Dolls was published on February 10, 1966. It remained on the *New York Times* Bestseller List for 28 consecutive weeks and was Number One on the Bestseller List of 1966. The novel is one of the top-selling novels of all time by a female writer, sharing the honors with *Gone with Wind* and *To Kill a Mockingbird*.

Pucci-clad media superstar!

Jacqueline Susann typed all her novels on a hot pink typewriter.

"And all you wanted was

1968

1965

a can of tomato soup!"

1968

1969

The Bugs Bunny Show
1960-1972

Top Cat
1961-1962

Jonny Quest
1964-1965

THE FAMOUS
ADVENTURES
OF MR MAGOO
1964-1965

The Alvin Show
1961-1962

The Atom Ant /
Secret Squirrel Show
1965-1967

ROGER
RAMJET
1965

Underdog
1964-1973

SPACE
GHOST
1966-1968

SPEED
RACER
1967

"Meet George Jetson,"

THE FLINTSTONES · 1960 - 1966 · FRED FLINTSTONE · WILMA FLINTSTONE · PEBBLES · DINO · BARNEY RUBBLE · BETTY RUBBLE · BAMM-BAMM · MR. SLATE · THE GREAT GAZOO ·

"WilllLMAAAA!"

"FLINTSTONES, MEET THE FLINTSTONES
THEY'RE A MODERN STONE-AGE FAMILY
FROM THE TOWN OF BEDROCK
THEY'RE A PAGE RIGHT OUT OF HISTORY
LET'S RIDE WITH THE FAMILY DOWN THE STREET
THROUGH THE COURTESY OF FRED'S TWO FEET
WHEN YOU'RE WITH THE FLINTSTONES
HAVE A YABBA DABBA DOO TIME
A DABBA DOO TIME
WE'LL HAVE A GAY OLD TIME!"

"YABBA DABBA DOO!"

George of
the Jungle
1967-1970

Wacky
Races
1968-1970

Scooby-Doo,
Where Are
You?
1969-1970

The Jetsons

1962 – 1963

"His boy Elroy, Daughter Judy, Jane his wife."

George Jetson

Jane Jetson

Judy Jetson

Elroy Jetson

Rosie the Robot

Astro

Henry Orbit
Cosmo S. Spacely
Mrs Starla Spacely
W.C. Cogswell
R.U.D.I.
(Referential
Universal
Differential
Indexer)

SPACELY SPROCKETS

"Jetson –
you're fired!"
Spacely

FOLK MUSIC

Simon and Garfunkel

Paul Simon, Art Garfunkel

"Sounds of Silence"

"Homeward Bound"

"I Am a Rock"

"Parsley Sage Rosemary and Thyme"

"The Dangling Conversation"

"The 59th Street Bridge Song (Feelin' Groovy)"

"A Hazy Shade of Winter"

"At The Zoo"

"Fakin' It"

"Scarborough Fair"

"Mrs Robinson"

"America"

"The Boxer"

"El Condor Pasa"

"Keep The Customer Satisfied"

"Baby Driver"

"Bridge Over Troubled Water"

Bob Dylan

"Blowin' In The Wind"

"Masters of War"

"A Hard Rain's A-Gonna Fall"

"Don't Think Twice"

"It's All Right"

"Talkin' John Birch Blues"

"When The Ship Comes In"

"The Times They Are A-Changin"

"The Lonesome Death of Hattie Carroll"

"Only a Pawn in Their Game"

"With God on Our Side"

"Mr Tambourine Man"

"Gates of Eden"

"It's Alright Ma (I'm Only Bleeding)"

"Like A Rolling Stone"

"I Want You"

"Just Like a Woman"

Joan Baez

"We Shall Overcome"

"Don't Think Twice"

"It's All Over Now Baby Blue"

"There But for Fortune"

"If I Were a Carpenter"

Peter, Paul and Mary

Peter Yarrow, Noel Paul Stookey,
Mary Allin Travers

"Blowin' In The Wind"

"Leaving On A Jet Plane"

"If I Had My Way"

"500 Miles"

"Where Have All The Flowers Gone"

"Lemon Tree"

"If I Had A Hammer"

"Puff The Magic Dragon"

"Tell It On The Mountain"

"This Land Is Your Land"

"Don't Think Twice It's All Right"

"Day Is Done"

The Seekers

Athol Guy, Bruce Woodley,
Judith Durham, Keith Potger

"I'll Never Find Another You"

"A World of our Own"

"The Carnival is Over"

"Someday One Day"

"Walk with Me"

"We Shall Not be Moved"

"Morningtown Ride"

"When Will the Good Apples Fall"

"Georgy Girl"

"Open Up Them Pearly Gates"

"Island of Dreams"

"Emerald City"

POP ART

Andy Warhol
The "father of Pop Art."

"Once you 'got' Pop, you could never see a sign the same way again. And once you thought Pop, you could never see America the same way again."

Warhol was responsible for the notoriously overused quote "everyone will be famous for fifteen minutes." This quote is often misused and should actually read "in the future everyone will be famous for fifteen minutes."

"I like to pretend that my art has nothing to do with me."

Roy Lichtenstein's distinctive renderings of comic books and advertisements drew on comic strips and everyday objects for inspiration, and his use of Ben-Day dots, lettering and speech balloons made his work instantly recognizable.

Famous for the use of repetitive images, including Campbell's Soup cans, Warhol's more well-known works are his silk-screens of Marilyn Monroe, Gumby, Coca-Cola bottles, Jacqueline Kennedy, Che Guevara, Chairman Mao and Elvis and his "Silver Pillows" and "Cow Wallpaper."

Between 1962 and 1964 he produced over 2,000 pictures in his "Factory."

A talented sculptor and filmmaker, he also produced the first record for rock band The Velvet Underground in 1967.

"The moment you cheat for the sake of beauty, you know you're an artist."

David Hockney's early work, such as "Tea Paintings" and "Love Paintings," which depicted consumer goods, gained him a reputation of a leading Pop artist – a label he rejected. His series on swimming pools and his 1964 "Man in Shower in Beverly Hills" are among some

Groovy chicks

Jean Shrimpton
"the shrimp"

Penelope Tree
"tree"

"The most beautiful girl
in the world."
ELLE MAGAZINE

"Her style is almost science.
Weird science that is."
JEAN SHRIMPTON

Lesley Hornby
"twiggy"

"The face of 1966." DAILY EXPRESS NEWSPAPER

Herb Adderley

1961-1969 Green Bay Packers. Named to Pro Bowl five times and played in four of the first six Super Bowls, becoming the first player in Super Bowl history to score a defensive touchdown in Super Bowl II in 1968.

Jim Brown

1957-1965 Cleveland Browns. Earned MVP honors four times, unanimous first-team All-NFL pick eight times, played in nine Pro Bowls in nine years, led NFL rushers eight years. Closed out his career with three touchdowns in 1966 Pro Bowl.

Dick Butkus

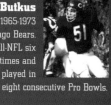

1965-1973 Chicago Bears. All-NFL six times and played in eight consecutive Pro Bowls.

"The Golden Boy" Paul Hornung

1957-1962, 1964-1966 Green Bay Packers. NFL Player of Year, 1960 and 1961, led NFL in scoring 1959-1961 with a record 176 points in 1960. NFL's Most Valuable Player in 1961.

Sam Huff

1956-1963 New York Giants, 1964-1967, 1969 Washington Redskins. Played in six NFL title games, five Pro Bowls, All-NFL three years. Redskins player-coach 1969.

In 1966 the NFL merged with the AFL and the first AFL-NFL World Championship Game, between the AFL-Champion Chiefs and the NFL-Champion Packers, was played in January 1967. The Packers won the contest, later renamed Super Bowl I, 35-10.

GREEN BAY PACKERS

Under head coach Vince Lombardi, the Green Bay Packers won the NFL title in 1961, 1962, 1965, 1966 and 1967, the first two Super Bowl's in 1967 and 1968 as well as six divisional championships.

"It's not whether you get knocked

BALL

CHAMPIONSHIP RESULTS

1960 – NFL: Philadelphia Eagles **17**, Green Bay Packers **13** / AFL: Houston Texans **24**, Los Angeles Chargers **16**

1961 – NFL: Green Bay Packers **37**, New York Giants **0** / AFL: Houston Texans **10**, San Diego Chargers **3**

1962 – NFL: Green Bay Packers **16**, New York Giants **7** / AFL: Dallas Texans **20**, Houston Texans **17** (OT)

1963 – NFL: Chicago Bears **14**, New York Giants **10** / AFL: San Diego Chargers **51**, Boston Patriots **10**

1964 – NFL: Cleveland Browns **27**, Baltimore Colts **0** / AFL: Buffalo Bills **20**, San Diego Chargers **7**

1965 – NFL: Green Bay Packers **23**, Cleveland Browns **12** / AFL: Buffalo Bills **23**, San Diego Chargers **0**

1966 – NFL: Green Bay Packers **34**, Dallas Cowboys **27** / AFL: Kansas City Chiefs **31**, Buffalo Bills **7** / SUPER BOWL I: Green Bay Packers **35**, Kansas City Chiefs **10**

1967 – NFL: Green Bay Packers **21**, Dallas Cowboys **17** / AFL: Oakland Raiders **40**, Houston Texans **7** / SUPER BOWL II: Green Bay Packers **33**, Oakland Raiders **14**

1968 – NFL: Baltimore Colts **34**, Cleveland Browns **0** / AFL: New York Jets **27**, Oakland Raiders **23** / SUPER BOWL III: New York Jets **16**, Baltimore Colts **7**

1969 – NFL: Minnesota Vikings **27**, Cleveland Browns **7** / AFL: Kansas City Chiefs **17**, Oakland Raiders **7** / SUPER BOWL IV: Kansas City Chiefs **23**, Minnesota Vikings **7**

down, it's whether you get up."

Vince Lombardi

Sonny Jurgensen 1957-1963 Philadelphia Eagles, 1964-1974 Washington Redskins. Regarded by many as the best passer of his time, won three NFL individual passing titles, surpassed 3,000 yards in five seasons, 300 yards in 25 games and 400 yards in five games.

Joe Namath 1965-1976 New York Jets. Best known for his $400,000 signing to the New York Jets in 1965 and his "guarantee of victory" engineering a 16-7 upset of the heavily favored Baltimore Colts in Super Bowl III. Rookie of the Year 1965, first quarterback to pass more than 4,000 yards in one season in 1967, AFL Player of the Year 1968, unanimous All-Pro selection with MVP honors in Super Bowl III 1968, named to all-time AFL honor team 1969, earned all-league accolades in 1967, 1968 and 1969.

Bart Starr 1956-1971 Green Bay Packers. Led the Packers to six division, five NFL and two Super Bowl titles. NFL Most Valuable Player 1966, MVP in Super Bowls I and II, three-time NFL passing champion and played in four Pro Bowls.

Johnny Unitas 1956-1972 Baltimore Colts. First- or second-team All-NFL choice eight years, All-NFL six seasons, NFL Player of Year three times, MVP three times in 10 Pro Bowls.

The Pink Panther 1964

Directed by Blake Edwards
Starring David Niven, Peter Sellers,
Robert Wagner, Capucine

Inspector Clouseau (Peter Sellers)
is a bungling investigator hot on
the trail of a burglar (David Niven),
who schemes to steal the rare
"Pink Panther" gem.

You only live

THE MIRISCH COMPANY presents

DAVID NIVEN
ROBERT WA

THE P
PANTH

TECHNICOLOR

with BRENDA DE BANZIE
COLIN GORDON and introducing
CLAUDI

"No, Cato, you fool!"

Peter SELLERS is in the Pink!

British actor and comedian Peter Sellers' first feature film was *Penny Points to Paradise* in 1951. It wasn't until 1959 however that he achieved success outside of the UK with his lead role in *The Mouse That Roared*. Sellers has been called a comic genius and his talents were demonstrated in a host of films in the 1960s, including: *Never Let Go* (1960), *Waltz of the Toreadors* (1962), *The Wrong Arm of the Law* (1962), *Dr. Strangelove or: How I Learned to Stop Worrying and Love the Bomb* (1964), *Casino Royale* (1967), and *I Love You, Alice B. Toklas!* (1968). Sellers married Swedish actress Britt Eckland, in 1964.

...so see the Pink Panther twice!!!

LKE EDWARDS Production

ETER SELLERS
R · CAPUCINE

...AMA

FRIES
RDINALE As the Princess

Screenplay by
MAURICE RICHLIN and
BLAKE EDWARDS

Directed by
BLAKE EDWARDS

MARTIN JUROW
HENRY MANCINI

The animated version of the Pink Panther was born when Friz Freleng and David DePatie were commissioned by Blake Edwards to create a cartoon for the opening credits of the film. Audience response was so positive that United Artists immediately commissioned 156 theatrical shorts. On December 18, 1964, *Pink Phink* premiered as a theatrical trailer. It won an Oscar® for Best Short Subject – Animated at the 1965 Academy Awards®. The cartoon series, consisting of three theatrical trailers linked by vignettes, premiered on NBC in 1968.

Henry Mancini is probably best-known for the distinctive musical theme he created for *The Pink Panther*, arguably the most recognizable piece of music of the 1960s. The original music to the 1964 movie was nominated for Best Music, Score at the 1965 Academy Awards®, and Best Original Score at the 1965 Grammy Awards.

A second Inspector Clouseau film, *A Shot in the Dark*, was released in June 1964. Also directed by Blake Edwards, Peter Sellers reprised the role of Inspector Clouseau alongside female lead, Elke Sommers.

scandinavian ikea geometric design white pine **tiki** faux bamboo **pop** inflatable furniture plastics pvc bean bags

palm trees thatched roof indoor bars cane furniture
fiberglass tubular steel **space age** ball chair bubble chair

"A Spoonful of Sugar"

"I Love to Laugh"

"The Perfect Nanny"

"Jolly Holiday"

"Step in Time"

"Fidelity Fiduciary Bank"

"Feed the Birds (Tuppence a Bag)"

"Stay Awake"

1964

"Sister Suffragette"

WALT DISNEY'S
Mary Poppins

JULIE ANDREWS · DICK VAN DYKE
DAVID TOMLINSON · GLYNIS JOHNS
HERMIONE BADDELEY · KAREN DOTRICE · MATTHEW GARBER
ELSA LANCHESTER · ARTHUR TREACHER · REGINALD OWEN
ED WYNN · BILL WALSH · DON DaGRADI
P.L.TRAVERS · BILL WALSH · ROBERT STEVENSON
TECHNICOLOR®

At the 1965
Academy Awards®
Mary Poppins was
nominated for 12
Oscars® winning:
Best Actress,
Best Special
Effects, Best
Original Music Score
and Best Song (for
"Chim Chim Cheree").

"Chim Chim Cheree"

Julie Andrews **as Mary Poppins**

Dick Van Dyke **as Bert Dawes**

"Let's Go Fly a Kite"

David Tomlinson **as Mr George W. Banks**

"The Life I Lead"

Glynis Johns **as Mrs Winifred Banks**

Karen Dotrice **as Jane Banks**

"Supercalifragilisticexpialidocious!"

Michael Garber **as Michael Banks**

th the sound of music"

"The Sound of Music"

"The Lonely Goatherd"

"I Have Confidence"

"Morning Hymn"

"Maria"

"Edelweiss"

"Sixteen Going on Seventeen"

"Alleluia"

"Do-Re-Mi"

1965

20th CENTURY-FOX presents

ROBERT WISE Production

RODGERS and HAMMERSTEIN'S

THE SOUND OF MUSIC

WINNER OF 5 ACADEMY AWARDS INCLUDING BEST PICTURE

Co-starring RICHARD HAYDN with PEGGY WOOD, CHARMIAN CARR, THE BIL BAIRD MARIONETTES and ELEANOR PARKER as "The Baroness"

Julie ANDREWS CHRISTOPHER PLUMMER

Music by Richard Rodgers · Lyrics by Oscar Hammerstein II · Associate Producer SAUL CHAPLIN · Directed by Robert Wise

Additional words and Music by Richard Rodgers · Screenplay by Ernest Lehman

Production Designed by BORIS LEVEN · Produced by Argyle Enterprises Inc. · COLOR BY DE LUXE · RELEASED BY 20th-FOX DISTRIBUTORS

"Something Good"

"So Long, Farewell"

"How Can Love Survive?"

"Preludium (Dixit Dominus)"

The real Maria von Trapp has a cameo role as an Austrian peasant woman in the background while Maria is singing "I Have Confidence."

"My Favorite Things"

The Sound of Music was nominated for 10 Oscars® at the 1966 Academy Awards® and won Best Director, Best Picture, Best Film Editing, Best Scoring of Music and Best Sound.

"Climb Ev'ry Mountain"

Julie Andrews as Maria

Christopher Plummer as Captain von Trapp

Eleanor Parker as The Baroness

Richard Haydn as Max Detweiler

Peggy Wood as the Mother Abbess

The Von Trapp Children: Charmian Carr (Liesl), Nicholas Hammond (Friedrich), Angela Cartwright (Brigitta), Heather Menzies (Louisa), Duane Chase (Kurt), Debbie Turner (Marta), Kym Karath (Gretl)

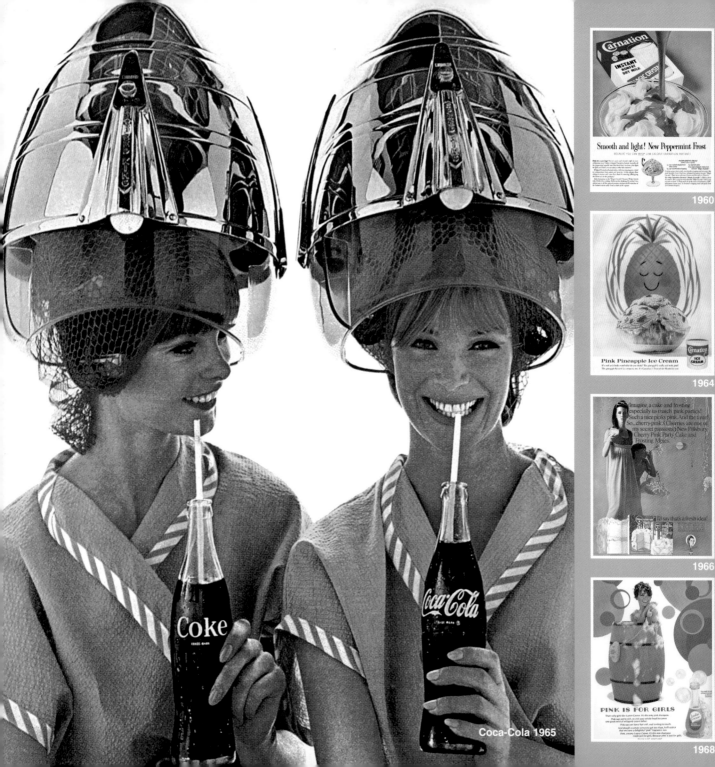

Smooth and light! New Peppermint Frost

1960

Pink Pineapple Ice Cream

1964

1966

PINK IS FOR GIRLS

1968

Coca-Cola 1965

"Pretty in pink!"

Tuttle Cottage Cheese, 1967

"Above all, have fun!"
Julia Child

Bon App

Julia Child's *Mastering the Art of French Cooking* was published in 1961.

"The French Chef" debuted on WGBH in Boston in 1963 and won an Emmy in 1965. 119 episodes aired between 1963 and 1966.

The French Chef Cookbook was published in 1968 and *Mastering the Art of French Cooking Vol. II* in 1970.

etit!

"The Galloping Gourmet,"
hosted by Graham Kerr,
broadcast 455 shows between
1969 and 1971 and screened
in 38 countries.

Known as the "James Bond
of the kitchen," Graham
Kerr was named "the most
dangerous man in the world"
by Weight Watchers.

Known to frequently "sip the
grape," Kerr's antics made
the *New York Times* on July 21,
1969. "Gourmet Sets Fire To
Dishcloth" shared the
headlines with "Man Sets
Foot On The Moon."

Mr. Magoo's Christmas Carol – 1962

Produced by UPA Productions of America, who produced the Mr. Magoo series of cartoons, the voice cast included Jim Backus as Mr. Magoo, Jack Cassidy as Bob Cratchitt, June Foray (who also voiced Rocket J. Squirrel, among others), and Paul Frees (the voice of Boris Badenov).

A Charlie Brown Christmas – 1965

On Thursday, December 9, 1965, "A Charlie Brown Christmas" was seen in more than 15 million homes, capturing nearly half of the possible audience, and was number two in the ratings, after "Bonanza." It won critical acclaim as well as an Emmy Award for Outstanding Children's Program and a Peabody Award for excellence in programming.

How the Grinch Stole Christmas – 1966

Directed and produced by Chuck Jones, with Boris Karloff as Narrator / The Grinch and June Foray (Rocket J. Squirrel) as Cindy Lou Lou, "How the Grinch Stole Christmas" screened on December 23, 1966. Thurl Ravenscroft, better known as the voice of Tony the Tiger, sang "You're a Mean One, Mr. Grinch."

Rankin Bass

Founded by Arthur Rankin, Jr. and Jules Bass in the early 1960s, Rankin Bass produced a large number of stop-motion and traditional animation movies, television specials and television series.

"Rudolph the Red-Nosed Reindeer had a very shiny nose, and if you ever saw it, you would even say it glows."

Rankin Bass' stop-motion Christmas specials are among their most popular productions and screen year after year to millions of viewers.

Rudolph the Red-Nosed Reindeer – 1964
Cricket on the Hearth – 1967
The Little Drummer Boy – 1968
Frosty the Snowman – 1969
Santa Claus is Coming to Town – 1970

Put a **tiger** in your tank.

Stronger than Dirt.

Take it off

Beanz

Ring around the collar.

Let Hertz put **y-o-u-u-u** in the driver's seat.

Think **small**

Because even an airline hostess should look like a girl.

Come **Alive!** You're in the Pepsi Generation.

Look, Ma, no **cavities!**

Only the crumbliest, **flakiest** chocolate,
Tastes like chocolate never tasted before.

Sch... You know who?

It sits as lightly on a heavy meal as it does on your

Lifts and separates.

Take it all off! The closer you shave the more you need Noxzema.

meanz **Heinz.**

Ladies, please don't **squeeze** the Charmin!

Does she or doesn't she?

Things go better with Coke.

Let your **fingers** do the walking.

Fly the **friendly skies.**

Go to **work** on an egg.

They like our girls, they like our food, they like our style.

When you got it, flaunt it.

conscience.

Aye yii yii yiiii
I am the Frito Bandito
I like Frito's Corn Chips
I love them I do
I want Frito's Corn Chips
I'll get them from you
Aye yii yii yiiii
Oh I am the Frito Bandito
Give me Frito Corn chips
And I'll be your friend
The Frito Bandito
You must not offend
Frito Bandito.

ACKNOWLEDGEMENTS

The copyrights of the images and text in Rose Colored: 60s are owned by the following individuals or organizations who have granted the publisher the right to use them. Every effort has been made to trace the copyright holders and the publisher apologizes for any unintentional omission. We would be pleased to hear from any not acknowledged here and undertake to make all reasonable efforts to include the appropriate acknowledgement in any subsequent editions.

Bullitt images from bfi and Getty Images; Psychedelia – Wes Wilson, Stanley Mouse, Rick Griffin, Victor Moscoso images © Ted Streshinsky/CORBIS, Art Spiegelman image © Roger Ressmeyer/CORBIS; Volkswagon advertisements from Volkswagen AG; Bewitched images from Getty Images; I Dream of Jeannie images from Getty Images; Alfred Hitchcock images from Getty Images; Martin Luther King, Jr. images from Getty Images; Green Stamps is a registered trademark of Sperry and Hutchinson, Inc.; Cleopatra images from bfi and Getty Images; James Bond images from bfi and Getty Images; Batman images from bfi and Getty Images; Rosemary's Baby images from bfi; Barbarella images from bfi; Robin and the Seven Hoods images from bfi and Getty Images; To Sir with Love images from bfi and Getty Images; The Beverly Hillbillies images from Getty Images; Gilligan's Island images and Getty Images; Splendour in the Grass images from Getty Images; Bonnie and Clyde images from Getty Images; Dick van Dyke Show images from Getty Images; Andy Griffith Show images from Getty Images; Westside Story images from bfi and Getty Images; Thunderbirds images from Getty Images; Lawrence of Arabia images from bfi and Getty Images; Jacqueline Susann – Pink Typewriter © Genevieve Naylor/CORBIS; Campbell's® Soup advertisements are the property of the Campbell Soup Company, all rights reserved; The Jetsons images from Getty Images; The Pink Panther images from bfi and Getty Images; The Sound of Music images from bfi and Getty Images; Coke is a registered trademark of The Coca-Cola Co. The French Chef images from Getty Images; The Galloping Gourmet images from Getty Images; Rankin-Bass images from Getty Images.

The publisher would also like to thank the following individuals and organizations for their assistance in the preparation of this book:

Ruth-Anna Hobday; Sonia Yoshioka-Carroll; Holly Stevens; Vibeke Brethouwer; Phil and Sheryl Vautier at ICE Design; Annie Matthee; Jenny Moore; Ana Vidovich; Birgitta Nilsson; Sean Neely; Les Krantz; Sarah McSkimming; Chris Hood; Nik Andrew; Ruth Hamilton; Jim Heimann; The British Film Institute; Steven Marinovich.

All other images Getty Images, www.gettyimages.com.

DVD documentary produced by Les Krantz, Copyright © 2004 Wildwood Films (Div. of Facts that Matter, Inc.).

Special thanks to Michael Fragnito and Susan Lauzau.

A BARNES & NOBLE BOOK

ISBN 0-7607-5952-9

Printed and bound in China by Everbest Printing Co Ltd

1 3 5 7 9 10 8 6 4 2

PQ